AF007625

English Handbook

Liz Heesom

Contents

Introduction

What is an 11+ English exam?	4
How to use this book	6

Comprehension

1	Recognising question types	8
2	Learning how to do comprehension	9
3	Identifying different question requirements	11
4	Defining words used in the text	14
5	Cloze tests	16
6	Recognising features of different text types	18
7	Checking your answers	20

Writing

8	Learning how to plan stories	23
9	Learning how to write stories	24
10	Checking your writing	26
11	Improving your writing	26
12	Watching the time	42
13	Other kinds of writing	43

Grammar and punctuation

14	Sentences	48
15	Phrases and clauses	50

16	Paragraphs	53
17	Commas	54
18	Other common punctuation marks	55
19	Word classes or parts of speech	60
20	Subjects and objects	73
21	Gender and diminutives	75
22	Synonyms and antonyms	76
23	Abbreviations and acronyms	78
24	Compound words	80
25	Direct and reported speech	81
26	Avoiding common errors: what NOT to do!	82

Spelling

| 27 | Improving your spelling | 86 |
| 28 | Learning awkward spellings | 88 |

Skills builder

English at home	106
English out and about	106
Working on English skills	107

Study guide	108
Glossary	111
Answers	116

Introduction

What is an 11+ English exam?

English is a test that often includes a comprehension (reading) paper, grammar, spelling, punctuation and sometimes a separate writing test. It is a common test for the 11+ exam. To be successful in the English exam requires fluent reading skills, a wide-ranging vocabulary, excellent spelling skills and a thorough understanding of the English language with its associated rules and patterns.

The 11+ exam is taken by children at the beginning of Year 6. It is a test used by state-funded grammar schools or by selective schools for Year 7 onwards. It is used to select the children who perform the best under exam conditions and to place them in a school environment with peers of a similar academic ability. Unlike most other exams, selective entrance tests cannot be retaken. There is no second chance at the 11+ (although some schools do still set exams for entry at 12+ or 13+), so there is often fierce competition to perform well and achieve good results.

There is one main exam board involved in producing 11+ English exams: Granada Learning (GL) Assessment. There are other exam boards and individual schools who write their own papers and some schools will have the 11+ exam completed on a computer rather than on paper.

An 11+ English paper can be written in two formats, following either a multiple-choice or standard layout. For a multiple-choice paper, children will need to choose their answer from a set of options and mark it on a separate answer sheet. Answers must be marked in these booklets very carefully as the answer sheets are often read and marked by a computerised system. In the standard format, children must write each answer directly onto the question paper.

As with most exams, 11+ exam papers are timed, typically lasting between 45 minutes and one hour. The introduction of a time-limit can potentially have an impact on a child's performance, so it is important for children to work through practice materials in both timed and non-timed environments.

The scope and content of an 11+ English test can often differ across UK regions, as there is a range of question types that can be included. However, a paper will generally be intended to test a child's ability to:read a piece of text or texts and answer questions on it

- scan, deduct, reason and justify
- write independently

- solve grammar and punctuation problems
- spot incorrect spellings
- read a sentence and answer questions on individual word meanings.

These skills are tested through a series of questions that include the following:

Comprehension

This is the ability to read a text or texts and understand information through the skills of scanning, deducting, inferring and justifying a response. Questions might include text types, true and false statements, ordering events and reasoning how and why an author has used literary effects. It also covers the ability to fit the correct words into gaps in a text.

Writing

This is the ability to understand different text types and to write appropriately for the text type asked for. Examiners look for a well-structured piece of writing that is coherent and logical, demonstrating a wide range of descriptive vocabulary, and strong skills in spelling, punctuation and grammar.

Grammar and punctuation

This is the ability to understand sentences, phrases, clauses, paragraphs, parts of speech and punctuation marks. Questions might include recognising word classes, plural and singular words, synonyms and antonyms, direct speech and reported (indirect) speech, and adding punctuation marks to a given text.

Spelling

This is the ability to understand spelling rules and exceptions. Questions might include homophones, root words, prefixes, suffixes and whether common spelling strings are correct. This is often done by reading a text and recognising where there are mistakes.

This book will help you to understand the key questions found in 11+ English exams. The Bond range of English assessment papers and the CEM English and verbal reasoning books can be used alongside this book to apply the information. The Bond series also provides a range of exam test papers in both multiple-choice and standard format.

How to use this book

The book has been divided into sections. How you work through the book is up to you. You can choose to work through the sections in order and complete the questions within them sequentially. Or if you prefer, you can choose any section to start and pick and choose a particular question type within that section.

Each numbered section includes an explanation of the particular question type and the skills that you will need to be able to answer the questions. Make sure you read through all the information carefully before attempting any questions and ask a parent or helper if you do not understand.

Checklists

For each question type, advice and checklists are provided to help you work through the questions and to aid your understanding.

Checklists will:

> ✓ contain all the main parts of the plot
> ✓ uncover the dilemma or problem
> ✓ explore the different persionalities of the characters.

Have a Go questions

These questions give you the opportunity to check your understanding of what you have just learned. For some of the longer questions, you might find it easier to do your working out on some spare paper.

> **HAVE A GO**
>
> Collect as many words as you can in your notebook where the masculine noun is different from the feminine noun. This particularly applies to jobs, animals and family members. If there is one, add the diminutive form as well.
>
> Here are some to get you started:
>
> *goose   fox   niece   waiter   cow   uncle   host   bride   pig*

In each section you will also find useful **Exam Tips** and important information that you should try to **remember** and apply when working through the questions both in practice sessions and in the actual test itself.

Glossary

Throughout the book important words and phrases that commonly occur in English test questions are included. You will find definitions of these words and phrases in the glossary at the end of the book. The glossary terms have been highlighted in black bold the first time that they appear in each section.

Top Tip!

It's a good idea to have access to a dictionary whilst working through the questions in this book so that you can look up new words that you meet and write down their definitions.

A note on question formats

The majority of 11+ exams now use multiple-choice answer format (where you choose your answer from a list of options). In Bond practice materials, some questions are multiple-choice and some require you to write or type the answer into a box, known as 'standard format'. We continue to use both because standard format questions are proven to be more effective for learning and practise, as having to decide on an answer yourself and the simple act of writing out your answer, make your brain work a bit harder and helps those important skills to get fixed in your memory, ready to be used when you sit down for the real test.

We hope you enjoy using the book. Good luck!

Comprehension

"I find comprehension difficult."

So do many people. You are not alone!

"What does comprehension mean?"

The word means *understanding*.

A comprehension exercise or test can consist of: a passage or passages of text; part of a story; a poem; a piece of information or explanation; a description.

Your job is to read the text and then show that you understand it by answering questions about it. Sometimes the text and the questions can be quite challenging. It can be difficult to understand anything at first.

You need to be:

- ✓ a good reader
- ✓ a good thinker
- ✓ a good word-spotter
- ✓ a good detective!

❶ Recognising question types

11+ English comprehension tests may have different kinds of questions. It depends on the school setting the test or the part of the country you live in.

Multiple-choice questions

This is where several possible answers to a question are given and you have to find the best one.

- Sometimes you underline the correct answer, put a mark in a box or mark a separate answer booklet.
- The answers can all look very similar so you have to find the right part of the text by **scanning** (looking quickly through the text until you come to the part you need) and then do your detective work.
- Never leave out an answer in a multiple-choice test. After all, the answers are all there and you have a good chance of choosing the right one if you make a sensible guess.

Standard questions

Here, the answers are not provided. You have to search the text carefully to answer the questions.

- Often you are asked to write the answers in complete **sentences**.
- Scan the text to find the right part for each question.
- Be careful to provide all the details the question asks for and write each answer in your own words. Usually, you will find all the information you need in the text.
- Look at the marks given for each question. These are often put in brackets at the end of the question. They can give you a clue about how much to write.

REMEMBER: In this book, whenever a new word about language is introduced, it appears like this. If you need to, you can check its meaning in the Glossary at the back of the book.

EXAM TIP

Some comprehension questions will have more marks available than others. To earn those marks, you will need to give a reason for your viewpoint or you will have to identify a range of true or false statements. Always check how many marks are available and how much evidence you need to provide.

2 Learning how to do comprehension

"How am I expected to remember a whole passage?"

You're not!

Comprehension is not a memory test. Even if the questions are on a different page or a different sheet, you must always use the text to help you find the answer, even if you think you can remember it.

"How do I begin?"

A useful **strategy** is to learn this five-point plan for doing comprehension.

1 Read the passage carefully, twice if you can. **Write nothing**.

2 Read all the questions through once. **Write nothing**.

3 Find answers to all the questions, using the passage to help you. **Write nothing**.

4 **Write** careful answers to the questions, in full sentences unless asked not to.

5 **Check** like mad!

REMEMBER: Never simply copy out chunks of text! You will lose marks. Try to use your own words unless the question instructs you otherwise. Sometimes you may need to incorporate a quote into your answer.

Of course, you may be taught other strategies or develop your own, but this five-point plan is a good way to start. It encourages you to read and think carefully before you start writing answers. This is especially important if the passage is long or difficult to understand.

"But there are words I don't know."

Yes, there may well be!

Sometimes you may have to explain meanings of words. These words are probably part of a longer piece of writing, so the text around an unfamiliar word may give you clues. Perhaps the word itself contains clues. It may contain a **root word** that you recognise or a **prefix** or a **suffix** that has a meaning. (See Section D.)

"I don't have any idea what one part of the passage means."

Always have a go, even if you are not sure. Read that **paragraph** several times, spot the key words and ideas and try to imagine what is going on. It's better to guess and put something, rather than leave a blank.

"I can't find the answer to the question anywhere."

To answer some questions you will need to 'read between the lines' or **infer** the answer. You will have to form your own opinion from the clues in the text and scanning won't help you here. For example, to answer this kind of question you may need to:

- **predict**, or imagine, what happens, or might happen, next
- give your opinion about why a **character** does something or acts in a certain way
- continue the passage in your own words as a piece of writing (see Section B).

In order to infer, predict or continue, it is very important that you are clear about:

- **who** the characters are
- **where** and **when** the passage is taking place
- **what** is happening: the **plot** or the **dilemma**
- **why** the passage is worth reading.

Who? – There can be one or more main characters and less important characters. Try to spot clues that bring the characters to life so that you can imagine them as real people.

Where? When? – This is the setting and explains the place and the time of the passage. Again, use clues to imagine what kind of place it is and the time of day or season.

What? Why? – The events are what make the storyline or plot. The plot can include main events and minor ones. The dilemma or problem is often the cause of most events. Be clear about what is going on and why.

3 Identifying different question requirements

You need several different skills to answer comprehension questions. Here are some examples of different question types and the **strategy** needed to solve each kind.

Obvious responses to the text

Finding

These questions ask you to find information from the text that is straightforward to find. Typical questions might be: *"How many children are there?"*; *"Where does the cat live?"*; *"When did Monet paint the picture?"*.

The skills required are:

- understanding what information is needed
- recognising key words in the question
- scanning the text to find the key words.

> **EXAM TIP**
> When you read a 'finding' question, underline the key words (names, dates, places). Make sure you know exactly what information you need to find. Often, a wrong answer is chosen because the question has been misread. Find the information needed and then copy the words used in the text for your answer.

These question types are often found at the beginning of a comprehension exam and are usually only worth 1 mark so it is important not to spend too much time on them. This is where scanning a text quickly is an important skill.

If the question begins with *"Who …"* look for a name.

If the question begins with *"Where …"* look for a place.

If the question begins with *"When …"* look for a day/date/time.

If the question begins with *"Why …"* look for a reason.

If the question begins with *"How many …"* look for a number.

Rephrasing

These questions ask you to read the extract and then to put some information into your own words. Typical questions might be: *"Describe the old man in your own words."*; *"What was the weather like? Use your own words to write about it."*

The skills required are:

- understanding the **vocabulary** used
- understanding how the words help to give feeling, description or atmosphere
- finding your own choice of words to help give the same meaning.

> **EXAM TIP**
> You need to find the section of the text referred to, underline the descriptive words in it, think of other words that would have the same meaning and rewrite the feeling, description or atmosphere.

Reasoned responses to the text

Deduction

These questions ask you to work out what has happened. You might think of them as 'because' questions. You are giving a *reason*.

Typical questions might ask you:

- *"Why did the deer run away?"* (because it was scared by the noise)
- *"How did the ship become damaged?"* (because it scraped against some rocks)
- *"Why was the café empty?"* (because it was a bank holiday).

The skills required are:

- understanding what information is needed
- reading the text carefully and thoughtfully
- finding reasons from the information given.

These question types can be worth more than 1 mark because the answer cannot be found through simply scanning for key words.

To give full answers to these kinds of questions, try to use **PE** or **PEE** to help you:

Point   Make a point.
Evidence   Use a short quotation as evidence to prove why your answer is right.
Explain   Try to explain in what way your evidence supports your answer.

> **EXAM TIP**
>
> The best strategy for answering these questions is to use the five-point plan and read the text really carefully. When you first read the text, it is a good habit to think like a detective about what you are reading and why something is happening. Look back at the text for the surrounding information as this may give you clues.

REMEMBER: Check that your answer is a 'because' answer.

Inference

These questions ask you to work out what might or could have been a reason for something to happen. As with deduction, you still need to think like a detective looking for clues, but you also need to think more deeply if the answer is not obvious.

Typical questions might ask you:

- *"Why do you think the boy cried?"* (The text says that he was tired and hungry and sometimes little children cry if they are tired and hungry.)
- *"Why did the queen feel disheartened?"* (The text says that the queen thought all the people would come to her party, but no one turned up. The queen was not expecting this so she felt disheartened.)
- *"Why did the cat take a short cut?"* (The text says that the cat was hungry, so to get home quicker, he took the short cut.)

The skills required are:

- understanding what information is needed
- reading 'between the lines' to find the meaning, if it isn't clear in the text
- thinking about **how** or **why** something might have happened using what information there is to make a good guess.

Did you notice that the responses above began with "The text says ..."? This is because you need to use information in the text to support your answer. The text becomes your proof or evidence to back up your answer.

Question types

Here are some typical question types. See if you can work out whether they are asking for obvious responses or reasoned responses to the text. You can then work out if they require finding, rephrasing, deduction or inference skills.

> **EXAM TIP**
>
> In many comprehension exams, these question types provide the maximum number of marks because you have to find reasons for your answer. Check the number of marks available and the wording of the question to find out how much proof you need to provide.

HAVE A GO

For each question, decide whether it is deduction (d), inference (i), finding (f) or rephrasing (r). Write d, i, f or r on the answer lines.

Be careful: there may be two possible answers.

a Explain why Jai felt tired. ....

b Tick the three false statements from this list. ....

Comprehension

c Describe in your own words the meaning of the phrase ....

d When was Mr Sasitharan born? ....

e Why did the nurse burst out laughing? ....

f Describe the house in your own words. ....

g How did the doctor feel and why? ....

h How did Tom change from the beginning to the end of the extract? ....

i Make a list of the items in the picnic basket. ....

❹ Defining words used in the text

There are a number of question types that look carefully at vocabulary.

- A **standard format** question might ask what a word means.
- A **multiple-choice format** might ask you to underline a word that means the same as a given word.

A common question is:

"What do these words mean as used in the text?"

It can be tempting to write down the meaning of the word if you know it, but this is a mistake. Many words change their meaning based on how they are used. Look at this example:

> *The escaped lion had come so close to her. It made her shaky just thinking about it and she needed the cup of strong, sweet tea to calm her nerves.*

What does the word 'sweet' mean as used in the text?

You may write down the word 'cute' and feel pleased. Of course, this is wrong because the woman didn't need a cup of strong, cute tea to calm her nerves. The correct answer for this word as used in the text is **sugary**. The woman needed a cup of strong, sugary tea to calm her nerves.

Always go back to the text and find the word so that you can give the meaning 'in context'.

Here are three different word definition questions to try out.

HAVE A GO

1 Read the following sentence and underline the correct answer.
   The football World Cup had teams participating from all over the world.
   What does the word 'participating' mean?

A	B	C	D
comparing	combining	contradicting	competing

2 Choose ONE word that is the best fit in this sentence from options A–D.

   Tam felt .... after eating too many chocolates.

A	B	C	D
sickening	starving	conspired	nauseated

3 Read the following text and add ONE word from the list below to each space so that the paragraph makes sense. Each word can be used only once.

   Tractors and farm .... now plough the ....,

   .... the seeds and gather the .... In times gone by,

   .... had to use .... and people to work the fields.

   animals   farmers   fields   harvest   machinery   sow

EXAM TIP

Your job in these types of questions is to choose definitions or organise which words go best in which spaces, so you need to read the text very carefully. Cross them off the list as you use them. If you don't know a word, try out the other words in turn in the context you are given until they make sense.

5 Cloze tests

In 11+ English you may come across **cloze tests**. These are a kind of comprehension test too. They are especially common in CEM exams (see p4 for CEM).

Cloze tests are where a text has a missing word or **phrase**.

Either you are given the words or phrases to add in the correct places, or you may have to think of a suitable word or phrase yourself. To solve cloze test exercises, you will need wide-ranging vocabulary skills, **grammar** skills and the ability to select the right word for the right place.

These are very similar to the word definition questions above and you can use the same kinds of strategies.

One strategy for solving this type of question is to read the list of words and then to read the text to get a clear idea of the **topic**.

Look for any clues. Try out words from the box in the gaps. Where do they make sense? Cross off the words as you use them.

Finally, read though the text to make sure it all makes sense.

Using the strategy above, see if you can do this cloze test.

HAVE A GO

1 Add the following words to the correct spaces in the text to make sense. Each word must be used only once.

   between   boarded   corridor   dismay   reserved   squashed   still

   As we .... the train to London, we noted with ....

   the number of people who were .... into every seat, every aisle

   and in every .... We moved .... carriages and

   .... we could not find a seat. I could have kicked myself for not

   having .... a seat, especially during the holiday season.

Another kind of cloze test is where you have to decide on a set of phrases and underline the one that makes best sense. This is a multiple-choice test. One of the choices will work but the others won't. For this kind of question, you have to know how the English language works, and the choices can be very similar.

Again, try out each phrase in the gap and choose the one that fits in the best in each case. Then read the text back to yourself.

HAVE A GO

2 Underline the correct phrases that fit into the spaces in the text so that the text makes sense.

Looking around at the dreadful mess, I [a] cried! I had never [b] so awful. Sticky blobs of syrup [c] the kitchen top and on to the floor.

a   [can of]   [can have]   [could of]   [could have]

b   [saw anything]   [seen anything]   [seed anything]   [see anything]

c   [drips off]   [drips of]   [dripped off]   [dripped of]

The third kind of cloze test is where you have to find a word of your own to fit into the gaps. This can be quite a challenge to many people. However, the text will be full of clues to help you.

Try using the same strategies as before to fill spaces with sensible words. Most of the time there will be only one possible answer that makes sense. Sometimes there may be a couple of possibilities. If more than one answer makes sense, you would get a mark for choosing one of these.

HAVE A GO

3 Find one word that fits into each space so that the text makes sense.

The . . . . loved looking after the animals. His father and his grandfather before him had owned the same breeds of cattle and sheep as he did now and he hoped one day that at least one of his own .... would take on the business. Waking up before dawn and watching the .... rise still thrilled him and at the end of the day when the sky was streaked with orange, pink and red, he felt pleasure at the thought of the following beautiful day. It was true that he worked extremely long ...., but this job was in his blood.

> **EXAM TIP**
>
> To do well in cloze tests, you will have to show that you are able to use words accurately, so it will be useful for you to go through the Grammar and Punctuation sections (pages 48–85) carefully before the exam. Make sure every word you put makes sense, and read the text to be certain of this once you have done the test. When there are gaps to fill, always put something, even if you are unsure, rather than leaving a word out.

6 Recognising features of different text types

Every text needs to be organised in some form of **layout**. In a comprehension exam you may be asked *"What type of text is this?"* or *"Where would you expect to find this extract?"*, so understanding the different text types is important.

You might be asked to find some examples to support your view, so you can show you can recognise common features of a text. Here are some ways in which you can recognise different text types.

Newspapers and magazines
- are factual and informative
- may use columns, **titles**, **subtitles**, quotations from people, numbers, photos, figures.

Poetry
- is imaginative and descriptive
- uses words to create **rhythm**

- might have **rhyme**
- uses literary **techniques** such as **alliteration**, **similes** and **metaphors**
- uses shorter lines, not free-flowing **prose**
- can be divided into lines and **stanzas**
- chooses vocabulary for effect.

Drama scripts

- have character names on the left and **dialogue** on the right
- don't use **inverted commas** for speech
- begin a new line whenever a different character speaks
- use stage directions and props
- can be divided into acts and scenes.

Diary entries

- are personal accounts written in an **informal** way
- have the day and date at the beginning of each entry
- may use short **paragraphs**.

Fictional prose

- tells a story through descriptive and entertaining writing
- can be divided into paragraphs, sections and chapters
- has characters or a **narrator**, and a plot
- could be a short story or a book.

Accounts and reports

- are factual and informative
- are usually organised **chronologically**
- may include facts, figures, graphs and charts
- may use lists, bullet points and a summary or conclusion at the end.

Reviews

- are factual along with the author's opinion
- offer a personal point of view
- look at the **positive** and the **negative** aspects
- have recommendations and a conclusion.

Instructions

- are step-by-step guides that tell you how to do something
- use bullet points or numbers
- use simple **sentences** with an **active verb** (usually in the **imperative** form) near the front of the sentence
- are always ordered chronologically
- may use pictures or diagrams.

7 Checking your answers

Most mistakes are made in the answers to the last questions in 11+ comprehension exercises, so check these extremely carefully! Try to remember these helpful hints when checking your answers:

- ✓ Look out for spellings, especially if any of the words you are using were in the passage.
- ✓ Be careful to punctuate accurately.
- ✓ Make sure the meaning of each answer is clear.
- ✓ Remember that there are clues in both the passage and the questions to help you answer correctly.

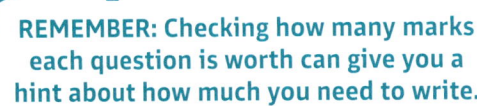
REMEMBER: Checking how many marks each question is worth can give you a hint about how much you need to write.

REMEMBER: the five-point plan! See page 9.

HAVE A GO

Here is a comprehension passage for you to read and questions to answer. Use the five-point plan to help you.

Make sure you read the introduction as well as the passage. There may be important clues here.

Look out for the different question types. There are 3 standard questions and 3 multiple-choice questions.

See how many marks each question can earn.

(Tom lives with his younger brother Sid at their Aunt Polly's house. He has arranged a meeting with his friend in the graveyard at midnight.)

At half-past nine that night, Tom and Sid were sent to bed, as usual. They said their prayers, and Sid was soon asleep. Tom lay awake and waited, in restless impatience. When it seemed to him that it must be nearly daylight, he heard the clock strike ten! This was despair. He would have tossed and fidgeted, as his nerves demanded, but he was afraid he might wake Sid. So he lay still and stared up into the dark. Everything was dismally still. By and by, out of the stillness, little, scarcely <u>perceptible</u> noises began to emphasise themselves. The ticking of the clock began to bring itself into notice. Old beams began to crack mysteriously. The stairs creaked faintly. Evidently spirits were abroad. A measured, muffled snore issued from Aunt Polly's chamber.

(From *The Adventures of Tom Sawyer* by Mark Twain)

1 How many people were in the house? ....

2 Why do you think Tom was in despair at 10 p.m.?

   ....

3 Write down five different sounds that Tom heard.

   ....

For questions 4–6, circle the correct answer, A B C D or E.

4 In the passage, 'perceptible' means:

A	B	C	D	E
easy to see	perceptive	recognisable	palpable	observable

5 Tom thought there were spirits abroad because:

   A small sounds made him think of ghosts.
   B he had heard stories of ghosts in other countries.
   C a bottle of spirits had been left on the table.
   D he had seen a ghost.
   E Aunt Polly was drunk.

6 Tom wasn't able to move about at 10 o'clock because:

   A his nerves were on edge.
   B he was afraid of waking Sid.
   C he had been forbidden to toss and fidget.
   D he was in despair.
   E he needed to wake Sid.

Writing

Most 11+ English exams will require you to show your writing skills and your ideas in a creative way. This could be called:

- a composition
- an essay
- a story
- a description.

It is difficult to say how many **titles** you will be given to choose from for this part of the exam. Sometimes you will have one or two titles; sometimes there will be a whole set of different options.

You may have to:

- write a made-up story or a factual essay based on a particular idea or from a given title
- write a description based on a picture, a place or a person you know
- write a letter
- read a short beginning and then finish the story yourself
- answer questions on a comprehension passage and then continue writing the passage as a writing test.

You always have a certain time to produce your writing. This could be between 30 minutes and one hour. Read the instructions at the beginning carefully, so that you know how much time you have. Then, remember to keep an eye on the time as you write.

"Why do I have to write something?"

Creative writing gives you a chance to shine. You can show off your:

- wide reading
- extensive **vocabulary**
- creativity
- enjoyment of language
- knowledge of what makes writing special
- fluency.

"How do I begin?"

To start with, let's think about writing stories. The other main kinds of writing will be dealt with later on in Section 13 (page 43).

8 Learning how to plan stories

Getting started is often the most challenging part!

That's where noting down a short plan can be very helpful. It will help you to organise your ideas and give your writing a **structure**.

First of all, think about these tips:

- ✔ Remember that you're going to write a short story, essay or description, not a book!
- ✔ Who is your reader?
- ✔ Keep your ideas simple.
- ✔ Always bear the title and instructions in mind.
- ✔ Think about who is going to tell (narrate) the story. You? Or one of the **characters**?

Next, using bullet points and key words, you could jot down:

- **Where**?   setting
- **When**?   time
- **Who**?   names of main characters
- **What**?   **plot**, **dilemma** or problem
- **How**?   solution

REMEMBER: Who are you writing for? (audience)

Why are you writing? (purpose)

"I don't like planning. I just want to write."

Everyone's different; some people really find it cramps their style to plan, and like to go with the flow of writing. That's fine, as long as you keep the structure or shape of your story going: beginning, middle, end.

For those who find it helpful to plan, the next stage of planning concerns **paragraphs**. These are the 'chunks' or 'stages' of your writing and, if you forget to use them, it is very difficult to do anything about it by the time you reach the checking stage. So, as part of your planning you need to develop your story in paragraphs, using bullet points to remind yourself of key words.

For instance, given the title 'Tunnel Adventure', you could:

1 First, plan a rough outline like this:

- **Where**? rocky seaside
- **When**? summer holidays
- **Who**? Ed and Joe, brothers
- **What**? explore, find tunnel, nearly get caught in rising tide
- **How**? swim to safety

2 Next, develop the plot in paragraphs:

- explore rock pools
- tunnel leads to possible treasure or pirates
- notice rising tide
- time is running out
- the solution

… or whatever you decide.

Your plan should remind you to begin a new paragraph for each new stage of your story. Of course, if there is **dialogue**, each time someone starts talking, you also need to start a new paragraph.

9 Learning how to write stories

It's down to business! You have learned how to plan your story. Now you need to start writing.

What are your aims when writing a story?

> ✓ **Think** about the title or the instructions – before you begin writing, as you are writing and when you check at the end.
> ✓ **Structure** your story. It needs a beginning, a middle and an end.
> ✓ **Organise** your story into paragraphs and sentences.
> ✓ **Entertain** your reader. There's no point writing something so boring it sends your reader to sleep!
> ✓ **Communicate** what you want to say to your reader clearly. Your spelling, grammar and punctuation must be accurate.
> ✓ **Write legibly**. Your reader needs to be able to read what you have written.

"But I can't think of anything to write."

Writer's block

Writer's block is a very common problem, not just for children preparing for exams. Planning should help you get started, but if you're still stuck, try the '**w w w w w w h**' trick. Each letter stands for a question word:

Where?   **When?**   **Why?**   **Which?**   **Who?**   **What?**   **How?**

It's sometimes called the 'journalist's trick', as journalists have to write on demand to keep newspapers full of stories. You, too, are writing on demand in an exam. You thought about some of these question words at the planning stage, but they come in useful at any time when you get stuck. Just ask yourself questions using these question words; your answers should help to get you going.

The beginning

You must try to grab your reader's attention from the very start, so welcome your reader in with a hook! You could think about how to:

- ✓ set the scene
- ✓ introduce at least one character
- ✓ give some hints about a problem that the characters will face later
- ✓ use interesting language to describe the scene and characters
- ✓ plunge into the story.

Get stuck into the story and try to enjoy it! The chances are that then your reader will too.

The middle

This is where the action happens, so keep up the pace. Remember, your time is limited!

The middle of the story could:

- ✓ contain all the main parts of the plot
- ✓ uncover the dilemma or problem
- ✓ explore the different personalities of the characters.

You are telling the story. You are the master magician and the pen or pencil is your wand!

The end

"I just write 'The End'."

This is where you bring your story to a close. It should be quite clear to your reader that your story has come to an end, so there's no need to write 'The End'.

For the ending of your story, which may be only one paragraph, you could:

REMEMBER: You need to write in paragraphs and your plan can help remind you.

If you use dialogue, each time a different character starts talking, you need to start a new line.

- ✓ find a solution for the dilemma or problem
- ✓ tie up loose ends – unless you want to leave your reader guessing by using a **cliffhanger**
- ✓ perhaps refer back to the title in some way, or explain the **moral** of the story, if there is one.

🔟 Checking your writing

All writers need to check what they have written. Professional writers pay proofreaders to do this job for them. You will have to check your work yourself, so always make sure you leave time to check your writing at the end.

It is important to keep at least five minutes of your writing time for checking. Practise reading out your writing to yourself, sentence by sentence. That way you can learn to check the first three most vital parts of this checklist:

- ✓ <u>sense</u>
- ✓ <u>sentences</u>
- ✓ <u>spelling</u>
- ✓ punctuation
- ✓ grammar
- ✓ interest
- ✓ vocabulary
- ✓ handwriting

⑪ Improving your writing

You have learned and practised how to give your writing a clear structure when planning and writing a beginning, a middle and an end. You have also thought about how to check your story. It is now time to think about how to improve your story writing in more detail.

Have a look at these four examples of children's writing. The children were shown this short picture story and asked to write an interesting and entertaining sentence for each picture. This isn't the type of exercise you will be given in an 11+ English exam, but it is very useful for recognising different kinds of story-writing.

Based on 'Greedy Mouse' from *Picture Stories by Rodney Peppé*

A

> One day Greedy mouse was very hungry so he went to look for some food. He found a piece of cheese on the flor. He ate some then he ate it all. and could not get back in his hole.

by Lily

This story has a beginning, a middle and an end, but it is very dull! You could call it a 'bare bones' story. It has all the structure, but is not entertaining or interesting for the reader. What could be done to improve a story like this?

Here's a different version of the same story.

B

> Greedy mouse
>
> Greedy mouses tummy was empty and he wanted a big bit of mouth watering cheese. He looked down the advertising hall way he could not go. that far because its boring the plum cat. Suddenly he saw a big bit of steaming cheese. He ate, ate, ate till it was all gone. He finally went to his hole but he was to fat to get in.

by Kai

You can see that Kai has developed the 'bare bones' writing that Lily produced by adding details, humour and more interesting vocabulary.

Writing 27

Here is a third version of the same story.

C

Greedy Mouse

1. Greedy Mouse was really hungry, as the hog family never left any crumbs at dinner.
2. "Hey look at that enormous piece of cheese!" Greedy Mouse thought out loud.
3. "Mmmm, yum, yum, yum," thought greedy mouse, "that was delicious!"
4. "Oh, no, now I can't get into my hole, but hey, at least there's that lump of cheese I haven't yet polished off!"

by Annabel

Here you can see that Annabel has added not only details, humour and interesting vocabulary, but also dialogue.

Finally, this version is developed even further.

D

The scrawley grey mouse was as ravenous as a street child.

He was scavenging for food about the castle when he came across the most mouth watering piece of cheese he had ever seen in his life.

In a split second he had eaten almost all of it like a vulture feeding on a dead elephant.

He was just finnishing the last bit when he let out a humungous yawn, he squeezed his head through, but he had eaten so much that mouse could no longer fit through his tummy his hole!

by Sophie

Sophie has really developed her vocabulary, by adding **adjectives**, details and **similes**, using **complex sentences** and thinking about the mouse's feelings.

You can make your writing more interesting too by using some or all of these ideas:

Ten ways to improve your writing
- ✓ bring your characters to life (page 29)
- ✓ add details (page 30)
- ✓ think about feelings (page 31)
- ✓ use adjectives and **adverbs** (page 32)
- ✓ develop your vocabulary (page 33)
- ✓ vary your sentences (page 35)
- ✓ include dialogue (page 36)
- ✓ add **imagery** (page 37)
- ✓ think about the senses (page 40)
- ✓ write clearly and legibly (page 41)

There is a separate section for each of these ten ways.

Bring your characters to life

Including just a few details about your characters can help your reader to imagine them more clearly. Try making a flow chart about a character like this:

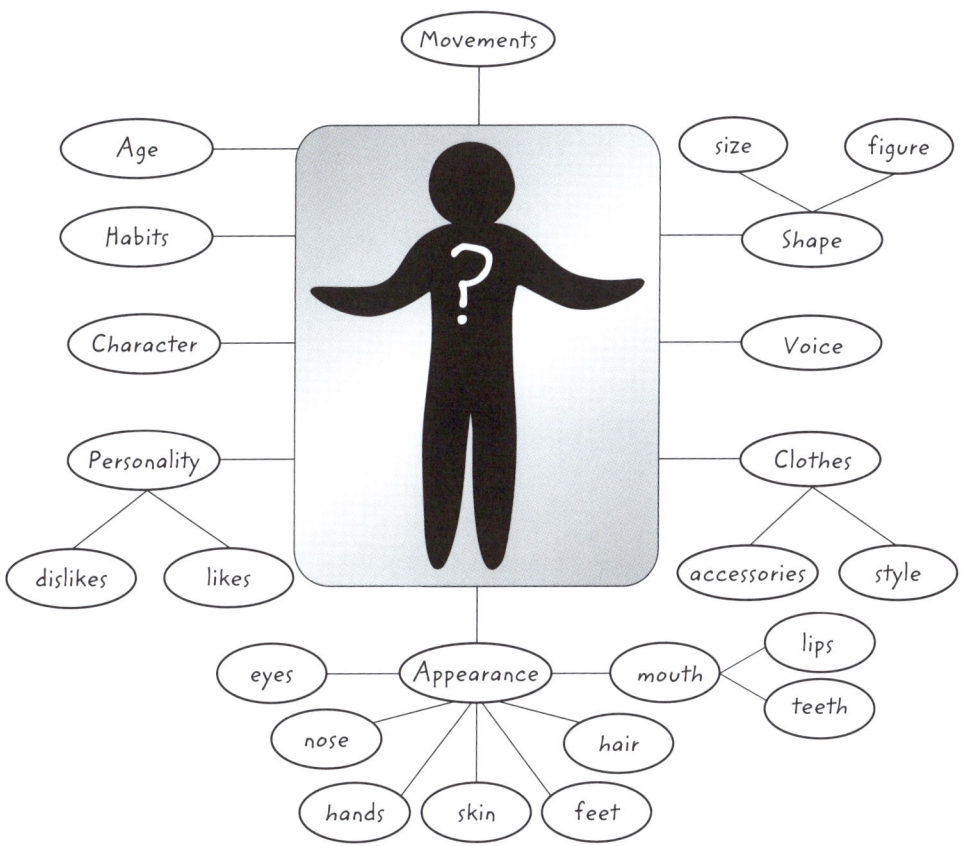

A useful exercise is to write two completely different sketches of the same character. This will help to show how different details can change the mood, personality and appearance of a character. Your reader will have a different opinion of the character too.

For instance, compare these two descriptions:

> 1. Chris shrugged his shoulders gloomily after his defeat, his lank hair drooping over his sullen eyes. "I never seem to win," he muttered.
>
> 2. Chris's entire face beamed, in spite of his disappointing defeat. "It was a brilliant game, even though I lost," he laughed, his black eyes sparkling through his mop of hair.

Notice how what Chris says helps to show his personality. Also notice how the details of what Chris looks like change the way you think about him.

HAVE A GO

1. See if you can if you can imagine completely different versions of a character, Musa, who has dropped his favourite pen on his way to school. Write two sketches, including details, mood, personality and dialogue to describe the different Musas.

   Try doing the same with other characters, like a dinner lady, a relative, a toddler, a teacher, a friend.

   Discuss what you have written with an adult for **feedback**.

Add details

When you are writing, you could just write a 'bare bones' story that has all the parts that make up a story (a beginning, a middle and an end) but is like a fleshless skeleton or a tree in winter. A 'bare bones' story is not likely to entertain or grab the attention of the reader. You would not really be using your imagination either.

You can develop a 'bare bones' story by adding adjectives and adverbs, more **complex phrases**, and more interesting and informative sentences.

You can also think of using techniques to emphasise, such as **alliteration**, **repetition** or **hyperbole** in your writing.

Alliteration is often used in poetry but can be very effective in descriptive writing too. Look out for when writers use a number of words that start with the same letter, for example: *It was wild, wet, windy weather* or *Swishing, splashing and swooping, six seals swiftly surrounded the boat.*

Using repetition can also be very effective to make pictures or ideas stick in the reader's mind. See how repeating the word 'fog' in this extract from *Bleak House* by Charles Dickens explains the effect of fog:

> *Fog everywhere. Fog up the river … fog down the river … Fog on the Essex marshes. Fog on the Kentish heights.*

It makes you feel fog in your bones!

Hyperbole is another form of emphasis, often used when talking, and can be quite amusing. Here are some examples of hyperbole:

It was raining cats and dogs during our outing.

I've told you a million times not to do that!

He'll be here in two seconds.

I had tons of homework last night.

HAVE A GO

2 See if you can transform this rather dull sentence using details.

The dog wagged its tail.

....

Discuss what you have written with an adult for feedback.

Think about feelings

Here are some examples of ways we can feel from time to time:

angry   delighted   jealous   excited   sorry   nervous

disappointed   sad   frightened   anxious   lonely   happy

It is easy to forget about including feelings when you are writing. Using them can help your characters to come alive. After all, different people react in different ways to things that happen.

You can collect many ideas by observing yourself and others in real life, as well as experiencing characters in books, films or plays.

For instance, feeling angry can make you:

- ✓ 'see red'
- ✓ want to explode
- ✓ shout and scream
- ✓ hide
- ✓ jump up and down
- ✓ say things you don't mean
- ✓ cry
- ✓ stamp your feet
- ✓ slam doors.

HAVE A GO

3 Jot down similar ideas for how you might feel or react if you were:

contented   scared   tired

Discuss what you have written with an adult for feedback.

Use adjectives and adverbs

Every sentence, even the most basic, needs a **subject** and a **verb**. The subject can be:

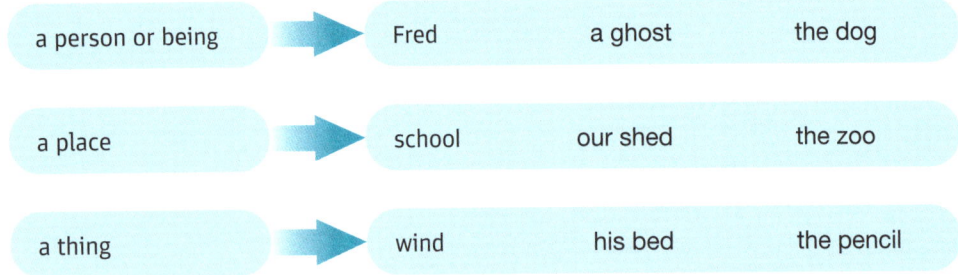

To make a simple **sentence** from these **subjects** you can add a **verb**:

Fred jumped.   *A ghost appeared.*   *The dog barked.*
School starts.   *Our shed collapsed.*   *The zoo opened.*
Wind whistles.   *His bed creaked.*   *The pencil snapped.*

As you can see, these sentences are so basic that they are pretty dull!

By adding adjectives or adverbs you can transform them in any way you like.

*Old Fred jumped **carefully**.*
*The anxious dog barked **frantically**.*

*An eerie ghost appeared **suddenly**.*
*His rickety bed creaked **alarmingly**.*

And so on …

Adjectives and adverbs add detail to the subject or object you are describing. By using them you can vary simple sentences in countless ways. So, if you include different adjectives and adverbs in your writing, you will make a story much more effective, vivid and attention-grabbing for the reader. (See page 32 for more information on adjectives and adverbs.)

HAVE A GO

4 Transform these very basic sentences in a similar way:

a
Our shed collapsed.

b
The zoo opened.

c
The pencil snapped.

See if you can write three or four completely different versions for each basic sentence in your notebook.

Discuss with an adult for feedback.

Develop your vocabulary

You may not realise it, but we all have hundreds and thousands of words floating around in our memories. Often, we only use a small number of them in everyday speech. The rest of our vocabulary (all the words we know) remains unused.

When you are writing, you need to show how you can choose appropriate words to build up a clear picture of what you want to say. This can make your writing more original and individual. What you want to say, and how you say it, is likely to be very different from what someone else would write.

Be interested in words!

The world around you is packed with words, so try to 'soak up' as many as you can!

REMEMBER: Your vocabulary is your word power!

Here are some ways you can learn new words:

- ✓ listen closely to other people talking
- ✓ read different sorts of books
- ✓ talk to lots of people: friends, family, teachers
- ✓ watch television programmes, films, video clips, plays.

You can even learn new words while playing computer games!

A dictionary and a thesaurus are also wonderful places to find out about words. Use a thesaurus to search for alternative versions of the most common or simple words that first spring to mind.

Words that have the same or similar meanings are called **synonyms**. (See page 76 for more detail on synonyms.) Using synonyms in your writing can help to avoid repetition. This can make a story more descriptive and more interesting for the reader.

One of the most common and overused words in English is the word 'said'. A quick look in a thesaurus shows that there are many interesting alternatives that can be used. (You may need to look up 'to say' as 'said' is the past **tense** of the **verb** 'to say'.)

For instance:

said → uttered, replied, laughed, declared, answered, cried, stated, mentioned, shouted, announced, observed, screamed, remarked, revealed, whispered

HAVE A GO

5 Here are four other overused words:

big   little   nice   went

There's nothing wrong with them, but there are many more interesting alternatives. Make a collection of as many alternatives as you can. To help you, think of a sentence containing each of the four words, for example:

There was a <u>big</u> machine digging up the road in front of where we live.

> A *little* parcel arrived in the post.
>
> We had a *nice* day.
>
> The old man *went* along the path with his dog.
>
> Try to think of as many alternatives to the four words as you can or use a thesaurus – there are lots!
>
> Keep adding to your list and try to use more interesting words in your writing.

Be brave! Try out new words in your writing but make sure you know what they mean, and how they are spelled, so that you can use them accurately.

Vary your sentences

> Ben went home from school. Then he went upstairs. Then he got out his Lego. Then he played with it. Then he had his meal. Then he went to bed.

We all used to write like this when we were first learning to write. All our sentences had the same shape and most began in the same way. You can see these are not very exciting sentences to read.

Understanding how to change the shape and length of sentences in different ways is an important skill that you need to show in your writing. Using a variety of sentences can help to make your writing more interesting for your reader.

You can transform sentences in all kinds of ways. You can:

- ✔ add adjectives or adverbs
- ✔ use more powerful verbs
- ✔ use **conjunctions** to join two or more short sentences together
- ✔ add **phrases** of time or place to the beginning or end of sentences
- ✔ change the order of parts of the sentence
- ✔ use **pronouns** like *who*, *which* or *that* to connect sentences.

See how the first sentences from the story about Ben could be transformed:

> Ben trudged home from school <u>and</u> went upstairs.
>
> <u>Nine-year-old</u> Ben plodded <u>wearily</u> home from school.
>
> Ben plodded home from school, went upstairs, got out his Lego <u>and</u> played with it.
>
> <u>At half-past three</u>, Ben arrived home from school, <u>past</u> the playing field.
>
> Ben went <u>upstairs</u> after he plodded home from school.
>
> Ben, <u>who</u> was really tired, trudged home from school, <u>which</u> seemed a long way.

Include dialogue

By including dialogue (**direct speech**) in your stories, you write down some of what your characters actually say.

REMEMBER: Dialogue is a conversation between at least two people.

Using dialogue can help to:

- ✓ break up your narrative (continuous writing)
- ✓ make your writing more lively
- ✓ make your characters more realistic and uncover more about their personalities.

Look at how part of the earlier, dull story about Ben can be changed into a livelier story by including dialogue.

> Ben plodded home from school. "I'm so very tired," he muttered. "I need a rest."
>
> His mother greeted him as she heard him come in.
>
> "Hello, love, how was your day?"
>
> "Fine," Ben replied as he went upstairs. He got out his Lego and built a fantastic spaceship. "Mission control to Mr Spock. Can you hear me?" he made the astronaut say as he whizzed the spaceship through the air.
>
> "Ben! Tea!"
>
> "I'm coming." Ben ran downstairs and into the kitchen.

In order to use dialogue, you must learn how to set out and punctuate speech.

Look again at the sections of dialogue in the story about Ben. What do you notice happens each time a different character speaks?

When writing dialogue, you must remember to:

- ✓ begin a new line or paragraph each time a different character starts to speak
- ✓ **indent** (or leave a gap) before starting to write a new line
- ✓ put **inverted commas** before and after the direct speech
- ✓ finish a question with a question mark
- ✓ finish a statement with a full stop
- ✓ finish an order, an expression of surprise or excitement with an exclamation mark
- ✓ use commas, where needed, to separate *what* someone is saying from *who* said it or the storyline.

HAVE A GO

6 Choose one of the sentences you varied and added to on page 35. Add some dialogue to it, remembering to start a new line and indent for each new part of a conversation.

Discuss what you have written with an adult.

Add imagery

A way of adding more interest and detail to your writing is to include imagery. Imagery creates pictures in the reader's mind by comparing one thing with something different. The two most common types of imagery are similes and metaphors.

Most people find similes easier to spot and to use than metaphors. The word simile starts like the word *similar*. Similes compare one thing with another by using the word *like* or the phrase *as ... as*.

Similes are a very effective way of describing something with few words but creating a vivid picture in the reader's mind. For example:

Her feet were **like** ice. This sentence uses something that the reader will recognise (ice) to describe the girl's feet. What comes to mind when you think of ice? Ice is very cold. So the sentence shows that the girl's feet were extremely cold, not that she had blocks of ice where her feet should be!

The giant was **as** big **as** a house. → This sentence compares the giant with something that the reader is familiar with (a house). By doing this, it allows the reader to 'see' or 'picture' how big the giant is, as he is described as being the same size as a house.

Many similes have been part of our language for centuries and it is important to know some of the most common ones. Here is a list of 15 of the most well-known ones:

as proud as a peacock	as busy as a bee	as light as a feather
as easy as pie	as brave as a lion	as cool as a cucumber
as fit as a fiddle	as clean as a whistle	as bright as a button
as dry as a bone	as bold as brass	as quick as lightning
as tough as old boots	as white as snow	as sly as a fox

Some of the most common similes can be overused, so try to think up some new ones. A new simile can really surprise and amuse a reader. Here are some examples to get you thinking:

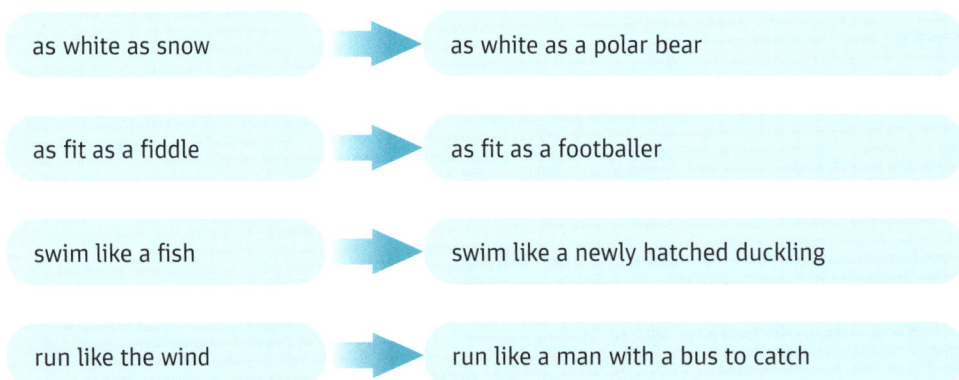

HAVE A GO

7 See if you can make up some more unusual and original similes for some of the ones on page 38. Try to think of things that you know from your own experience because this will help to make the similes more original, interesting and personal.

Discuss them with an adult for feedback. Make a game of creating new similes in your family. Spot good ones in your reading.

Metaphors suggest similarities between two things but they do not make direct comparisons in the way that similes do. They describe something as if it were something else.

For instance, here are two simple sentences:

John lost his temper.   *The spider's web was covered with dew.*

Look at how these sentences can be changed by using metaphors:

John's temper **boiled over**.

The phrase 'boiled over' is more commonly used to describe water that has reached its boiling point and is now frothing over the side of a saucepan, trying to push the lid up. This is the image that is created when we read the sentence about John. It shows that John is so angry that he is about to explode!

The spider's web was covered with **diamonds**.

Diamonds are precious gems that sparkle in the light. They are not found on spiders' webs, so this sentence shows that something else on the spider's web was sparkling. As spiders' webs are often found in gardens or hedgerows, it is likely that droplets of water (or morning dew) are being described here.

Metaphors can be more challenging to think of than similes when you are writing, but they can be used very effectively to help your reader create a picture of what you are describing. Again, spot metaphors in your reading, make collections and practise using some in your writing.

Another kind of imagery is **personification**. You can see the word 'person' in personification. This is when objects or other things are given human features or characteristics. Examples of this could be describing the sea as 'tumbling playfully onto the pebbles' or a tree as 'dancing and gyrating with glee in the stormy wind'.

Look out for examples of personification in your reading or in cartoon films, for instance.

Think about the senses

We discover everything around us through our five senses. We do this by:

seeing   feeling   hearing   smelling   tasting

So what have these got to do with writing?

You can help your reader to really experience what you are writing about by using words that appeal to some or all of the five senses.

Most of what people write relates to what they see in their mind's eye. This encourages the reader to use their sense of sight.

Adding dialogue or describing sounds can introduce the sense of hearing.

By including other sense words in your descriptions, you can also appeal to the reader's sense of touch, taste and smell.

The table below gives examples of five words for each sense. See how many more sense words you can collect.

Sight	Touch	Hearing	Smell	Taste
blue	*icy*	*clash*	*sickly*	*sour*
shiny	*scalding*	*patter*	*pungent*	*bitter*
enormous	*rough*	*boom*	*aromatic*	*spicy*
glittering	*smooth*	*soothing*	*fishy*	*delicious*
cloudy	*sticky*	*loudly*	*overpowering*	*sharp*

In writing, you can think of a 'sixth sense'. You can feel with your sense of touch, using your fingertips, but you can also feel with your heart. (See the section Think about feelings on page 31.) Describing characters' feelings can appeal to the reader's sense of emotion.

Here are some activities that will help you think about your senses when you write:

> ### HAVE A GO
>
> 8. Try describing a place by using all of your senses.
>
> 9. Choose an object from your room and write a description of it, without telling what the object is. Try to include all of your senses. Can someone else guess what it is?
>
> 10. Write about an action like peeling an apple, running in a race or playing an instrument and include all of your senses.
>
> 11. Shut your eyes and listen for a few minutes. Note down everything you heard.
>
> 12. Close your eyes and feel the different textures of the objects around you. Can you think of words to describe what they feel like?
>
> 13. Think about the four seasons and find sense words for each one.
>
> 14. Collect powerful **onomatopoeic** words which can be used to imitate sounds, such as:
>
>   tick-tock   splash   twittering   stomp   crash
>
>   Comics are good places to find examples of **onomatopoeia**.

Write clearly and legibly

If no one can read what you have written because it is not clear, is poorly spelled, badly punctuated, or doesn't make sense, then it's not worth writing! Take trouble over your handwriting. Learn to check (called proofreading) so you can correct any mistakes and improve what you write.

Look back at the list in the box on page 29 to remind yourself of the ten ways to improve your writing.

REMEMBER: It is useful to write in pencil when you are practising for 11+ English. This allows you to correct mistakes and make sure your writing can be easily read.

- ✔ Which of these do you use already?
- ✔ Which do you forget to use?
- ✔ Practise these ways as often as you can in your writing.

> **EXAM TIP**
>
> During the months before the exam, keep an exercise book to collect interesting sentences, descriptive phrases, writing ideas, dialogue that you have heard and favourite words, and jot them all down to build a collection of writing 'ingredients'. Check through your book frequently so that you can go into your exam remembering examples of what you have collected. These will add richness to your writing and may prove useful and time-saving.

12 Watching the time

"I'm hopeless at writing with a time limit."

You will always have a set amount of time to produce your writing in an 11+ English paper, because this is a test and to make a test fair, everyone has the same amount of time. It depends on who sets the test, but the whole exam is likely to last about one hour. You may only have half an hour to complete the writing task.

Many people, even if they enjoy writing at their own pace, find the thought of writing under timed conditions quite daunting. However, there are ways of helping yourself to use your time well.

- ✓ Practise your writing skills whenever you can. You will be writing at school, but you also need to practise at home. During Years 5 and 6, before you do the 11+ exam, you will need to try writing under exam conditions.
- ✓ Make sure you know where the clock is before you start. This is important when you are practising, and in the exam itself.
- ✓ Before you start, check how long you will have for your writing test.
- ✓ Allow about five minutes to plan your writing.
- ✓ When you are about halfway through your writing, have a quick look at the clock. This will help you to pace yourself for the second half.
- ✓ Leave about five minutes at the end to check your writing.

Don't worry if you don't finish your practice writing in the time limit to begin with. Put a mark next to the point you had reached when the time ran out and then complete your writing. The mark will show you how far away you were from the end when the time was up.

REMEMBER: There will always be a time limit!

If the time does run out before you finish, think about which sections took the longest to write.

- Were all those details necessary?
- Could you have moved the story on faster and saved some time?

Thinking about these questions will help you learn how to pace yourself while you write.

"How much do I need to write?"

It isn't easy to say exactly how much you should be able to write in a given time limit as:

- everyone's handwriting is different
- some people are very fluent and can write many pages in a short time
- some people prefer to plan and think first, so have less time to write
- some people get writer's block and can't think of very much to write.

A useful guide is to try to write a page and a half in an exercise book in half an hour. This is a very rough guide, though. Always remember: it is *quality* not *quantity* that is most important.

Another useful guide is to aim to write one beginning paragraph, three or four middle paragraphs and an end paragraph. Again, this is a very rough guide to remind you of the structure of your writing. It depends what kind of writing you are doing.

> **EXAM TIP**
> 1 Plan in paragraphs before you write.
> 2 Keep your ideas simple.
> 3 Remember the title.
> 4 Use a clear structure.
> 5 Develop your vocabulary.
> 6 Use full sentences.
> 7 Communicate clearly.
> 8 Entertain your reader.
> 9 Write legibly.
> 10 Watch the time.

REMEMBER: Everyone can improve with practice, as long as they get feedback and act upon it.

⑬ Other kinds of writing

Essays

In 11+ English, an essay is a piece of writing where you are discussing a title. It could be a personal **topic** like 'My Friends', 'Pets I Know' or 'My Hobbies'. It could be something general like 'Hunting Foxes: For and Against' or 'The Advantages and Disadvantages of a School Uniform'. This kind of essay can be called **persuasive writing** because you are trying to persuade your reader to agree with one point of view.

It may be useful to think of an essay title as being like a nut, which you need to crack open in your first paragraph. You need to show you understand what that title is about and what key words like 'Friends', 'Pets', 'Hobbies', 'Hunting' and 'School Uniform' mean.

Next it may be useful to put the title in the dock, as if in a trial. That way you can think of calling up your 'witnesses' to 'give evidence' and provide your opinions for and against the title. This can help give your writing a structure. A useful way to do this is to use phrases such as 'Firstly … secondly …' or 'On the one hand … On the other hand …' to begin your paragraphs and make your points.

It is very important that you keep the title in mind all the time and not let yourself go off onto a different **subject**.

Towards the end, imagine the judge summing up the evidence at a trial, drawing all the threads together and coming to a conclusion. This will be your final paragraph.

Letters

You may be asked to write a letter in 11+ English. This could be a **formal** or an **informal** letter. Remember, there are certain things to include in all letters:

> ✔ write the address and the date at the top of the letter on the right-hand side
> ✔ write in the **first person**, using *I* or *we*
> ✔ write in the present tense (usually).

Formal letters

Formal letters can be written for many reasons. You may be asking for information, complaining about something or explaining something. All formal letters should follow a particular format so, whatever your reason for writing, you should:

> ✔ put your name, address and the date clearly at the top of the letter on the right-hand side
> ✔ start with 'Dear' and the person's name, or write 'Dear Sir/Madam' if you don't know his or her name
> ✔ write in paragraphs:
>   - in the first paragraph, explain why you are writing
>   - in the middle paragraphs, add further details
>   - in the final paragraph, draw the letter to a close and perhaps ask for a reply
> ✔ use formal words and be firm
> ✔ use a formal ending:
>   *Yours sincerely* if you know the name of the person you are writing to or
>   *Yours faithfully* if you don't.

Informal letters

An informal letter is one sent to family members, friends or penfriends, for example. You can choose how to set it out and how you write it. If you are asked to write an informal letter in an exam, it is still important to write clearly and pay attention to sentences, spelling and punctuation.

- ✔ You can start with 'Dear', but could choose other, friendlier greetings, such as *Hello* or *Hi*.
- ✔ Follow this with the person's name.
- ✔ You could write in one paragraph.
- ✔ You could use informal words and a chatty tone.
- ✔ Finish with an informal ending, such as *Love from …*, *Bye for now*, *Best wishes*, *Write soon*.
- ✔ You may include a postscript (PS) to add something you forgot to mention in the letter.

Here are some ideas of the sorts of letters that you could be asked to write in 11+ English.

- Write to the Prime Minister explaining why children should have less homework.
- Write a letter to the town council arguing that your playing field should not be built on.
- Write a first letter to a new penfriend.
- Imagine you are on a week's adventure holiday. Write to a friend about your experiences.

REMEMBER: Before you start, work out whether the letter you have to write is formal or informal.

Features of formal and informal writing

Formal writing does not have any **contractions** (words using an **apostrophe** to show missing letters such as *don't*, *I'm* and *wouldn't*). It is not personal or expressive, and it is not chatty. It does have correct spelling, grammar and layout. You use formal writing when you want to be respectful to the target reader, such as a teacher, the editor of a newspaper or someone in authority.

Informal writing is the opposite. It is personal and expressive, can be chatty and allows for less formal grammar and layout. You use informal writing when you are leaving messages, or sending personal emails and texts to friends and family.

Here are two examples showing formal and informal writing structures:

> It is with regret that Rebecca Crane will be unable to attend the party on Saturday 3 March. She has a prior appointment that cannot be rearranged.

> Sooooo sorry but Becca can't come to the party as she's staying with her nan that weekend.

Recounts, reports and accounts

Recounts are used to 'retell' something. They can be personal, like a report about a school trip or a holiday, or impersonal, like a newspaper article or an account of an historical event.

In your 11+ English paper, you could be asked to write a description of an event or an experience you have had. You could be asked to write a report of a school summer fair for the school magazine, or perhaps an account of your last holiday, a trip abroad or a class outing.

When writing a recount, try to write as if you are telling the story of what happened. All recounts should be written in the past tense and they usually:

- ✔ start with an **introduction**, explaining what the writing is going to be about
- ✔ are written in the first or **third person** (*I/we* or *he/she/they*)
- ✔ have an organised structure, written in paragraphs
- ✔ use time **connectives**: *first, then, next, after, finally*
- ✔ retell the events in the order they happened (**chronologically**)
- ✔ include technical terms if the topic needs them
- ✔ include details to make the retelling lively
- ✔ end with a closing sentence or paragraph that comments on the event or experience.

EXAM TIP

In a writing exam, you will be given marks for interesting descriptions and the ability to use good words to show meaning. You may think of writing a fabulous story with lots of twists and turns, but, in reality, you don't have a lot of time, so a much simpler plot with well-described detail could gain far more marks. Although it is important to include plenty of detail in your writing, try not to put in so much that your meaning becomes lost.

HAVE A GO

Here are some ideas for different kinds of writing to try.

1. Write a short essay called: Is it important to have rules at school and at home?

2. Write a formal letter to the local council protesting about new houses being built on your school playing field.

3. Write an informal letter to a grandparent or other relative, telling him or her about a recent holiday.

4. Write an account of the last outing your class went on for the school magazine.

5. Write a report of a recent football or netball match, or other competition that you watched or took part in.

Ask an adult for feedback on what you have written.

Grammar and punctuation

"Those are the worst."

Both these parts of 11+ English tests can fill many children with alarm. What are they about?

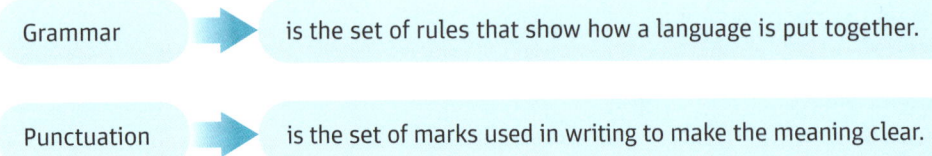

You are already an expert on **grammar**. Amazingly, you learn to speak grammatically when you first start talking and then get better as you chat, watch TV, listen to stories and 'bathe' in your language.

If English is not your first language, then do plenty of 'bathing' in English! Immerse yourself in all aspects of it. Reading all sorts of different things and paying attention to what you read is the best way.

For 11+ English, you need to understand:

- **sentences**
- **phrases** and **clauses**
- **paragraphs**
- commas
- other common punctuation marks
- **word classes** or **parts of speech**
- **subjects** and **objects**
- **gender** and **diminutives**
- **synonyms** and **antonyms**
- **abbreviations** and **acronyms**
- **compound words**
- **direct speech** and **reported speech**.

Each of these elements has a section of its own here. Read through any of the **topics** you need to brush up on.

There is also a section on common grammar mistakes and what to do about them.

14 Sentences

"Whenever I take a big breath, I put a full stop."

This is quite a good way of starting to write in sentences. It will usually sound wrong if you take a large breath in the middle of a sentence. It can also be useful to check through a piece of your writing, sentence by sentence, noticing when you need to take a breath before carrying on. It is likely you will need to put a full stop in these places. In order to be sure, though, you need to know what a sentence is and what different kinds of sentences there are.

Here are some useful checklists about **sentences**.

A sentence:

> REMEMBER: A sentence is a group of words that express a complete action or idea.

- ✓ starts with a capital letter
- ✓ must contain a verb (see page 32)
- ✓ usually contains a **subject** (see page 32)
- ✓ ends with a full stop, question mark exclamation mark, or an **ellipsis**
- ✓ is complete.

There are many different kinds of sentences. Here are some of the main ones:

- a statement: *He is getting out of bed.*
- a question: *Is he out of bed yet?*
- an order or command: *"Get out of bed, now."*
- an exclamation: *"What a way to start the day!"*

> REMEMBER: Question marks (?), exclamation marks (!) and ellipses (...) are special types of punctuation marks that can end sentences.

You need to be aware that a **sentence** can be:

- ✓ short: two or three words, for example: *Josh wailed.*
- ✓ long: often these are shorter sentences joined together with **conjunctions**: *Josh wailed because he had fallen down and cut his knee.*

Good writing will usually have a mixture of different sentence lengths.

You also need to recognise that a sentence can be:

- ✓ **single-clause** or simple: made up of only one **clause** (see page 50): *Josie played the recorder.*
- ✓ **multi-clause** or **complex**: made up of more than one **clause** or **phrase** (see page 50): *Josie played the recorder in the concert, while Anish accompanied her on the piano and the choir sang.*
- ✓ **active:** someone or something is doing something: *Josie played her recorder in the concert.*
- ✓ **passive**: something is being done to someone or something: *The recorder was played by Josie in the concert.*

Grammar and punctuation

Notice where sentences start and stop and look out for all of these sentence types in your reading.

"I can spot sentences when I read but I forget about punctuation when I'm writing."

This happens because you are telling yourself what you want to write in your head first, and we don't put punctuation marks in our thoughts. What we say flows from sentence to sentence. The punctuation is not obvious and sentences merge into one another.

You can tell when sentences stop and start from their sound, though. There are separate things you want to say, and each separate thing is a sentence. Listen to people talking and see where you think the full stops should go. By becoming aware of sentences as you read, you can also check your own writing for sentences. All it takes is practice!

REMEMBER: If your sentences have capital letters at the beginning and full stops, question marks or exclamation marks at the end, then you are already coping with the most important aspects of punctuation.

REMEMBER: If you are able to write down in sentences what you make up in your head, then the chances are that your grammar will be correct.

15 Phrases and clauses

"I'm never sure what the difference is between these two."

Many people don't find it that easy to tell the difference between phrases and clauses. These checklists and examples should help to make the differences clear.

A phrase is a group of words that:

- ✓ makes sense
- ✓ does not contain an active verb
- ✓ is not complete.

REMEMBER: Sentences are made up of phrases and clauses.

You need to be able to recognise phrases as being part of a sentence.

Here are some examples:

| the long way home | under his coat | over the moon |

Grammar and punctuation

A clause is a group of words that:

- ✔ contains a subject and an active verb
- ✔ is complete.

> REMEMBER: There are two types of clause: a main clause and a subordinate clause.

A **main clause**:

- ✔ makes sense on its own as a complete sentence.

Here are some main clauses using the phrases above:

we went the long way home   *he'd hidden it under his coat*   *she was over the moon*

A **subordinate clause**:

- ✔ does *not* make sense on its own
- ✔ starts with a **connective**: 'since', 'when', 'after', 'as', 'although'
- ✔ can be written before, in the middle of or after a main clause
- ✔ adds information to the main clause
- ✔ is separated from the main clause by a comma only when it begins the sentence.

If you put main and subordinate clauses together, you can make multi-clause or **complex sentences**.

Here are the main clauses from above, with examples of subordinate clauses (which are underlined) attached:

<u>After the concert ended</u>, we went the long way home.
He'd hidden it under his coat <u>when Reuben wasn't looking</u>.
<u>Although she had school the next day</u>, she was over the moon.
You need to be able to recognise main and subordinate clauses and use them in your writing.

LEARN: An **idiom** is a phrase that is often used to mean something that is not the same as the actual words. So 'over the moon' means delighted, not 'in a spacecraft travelling round the moon'.

HAVE A GO

1 Are these phrases (p), main clauses (mc) or subordinate clauses (sc)?

Label them with p, mc or sc.

a even though he left on time ....   f next to the door ....

b a group of words ....   g since it was a beautiful day ....

c as it was raining ....   h under the bridge ....

d the sun was shining................   i she bought three cars ....

e a green dragonfly ....   j the youngest was Charlie ....

Look at how these short, simple sentences can be transformed by adding phrases or clauses.

> *Jim was swimming. The water was freezing. He dived. His head grazed the bottom.*

- You could join them all together with conjunctions to make one long sentence:

   Jim was swimming <u>and</u> the water was freezing <u>so</u> he dived <u>but</u> his head grazed the bottom.

- You could add phrases to extend the shorter sentences:

   <u>Lulu's eight-year-old cousin</u> *Jim was swimming. The water* <u>in the crystal-clear pool</u> *was freezing.* <u>Taking a deep breath</u>, *he dived down to even colder water.* <u>All of a sudden</u>, *his head grazed the bottom.*

- You could add clauses to the short sentences by using conjunctions or connectives (underlined):

   Jim was swimming <u>while</u> his dad was fishing. <u>Although</u> the sun was shining, the water was freezing. He took a deep breath <u>and</u> dived. <u>Even though</u> the pool was deep, his head grazed the bottom.

Study sentences carefully as you read. Notice how phrases and clauses are used and practise using them correctly in your own writing.

HAVE A GO

2 Here are four simple single-clause sentences:

A butterfly fluttered by. It settled. Its wings quivered. Another one joined it.

In your notebook, try to do the following:

a Join the sentences into one longer sentence.

b Extend each sentence by adding phrases.

c Add extra clauses to each sentence.

Which version do you prefer? Discuss your sentences with an adult for feedback.

EXAM TIP

Always read through what you have written, sentence by sentence, to check that your sentences are clearly shown and they don't run together. Think about your reader.

16 Paragraphs

"Paragraphs are four or five lines of writing in a story."

Some teachers may encourage you to write in paragraphs following rules like this. However, if you look at paragraphs in books, you will see that they are all different lengths. There is no limit to the number of paragraphs a piece of writing can have.

Paragraphs are a form of punctuation. They show how sentences are grouped together. Using paragraphs makes your writing easier to read because they break up a piece of writing into sections or stages.

A new paragraph:

- ✓ starts on a new line
- ✓ is often **indented** (with a space between the **margin** and the first word) or, if the first line is not indented, a **line space** is left between paragraphs
- ✓ may come after a line space in a text, not indented, often in non-fictions texts or when first learning to write in paragraphs
- ✓ shows a change in subject or aspect: a new place, time or person
- ✓ is used in writing **dialogue**, each time a **character** has a turn talking.

Look out for how and when paragraphs are used in your reading. Practise using them in your own writing. (See Learning how to plan stories, page 23.)

EXAM TIP

In an exam, remember to plan in paragraphs before you start writing so that the stages of your writing are clear to your reader.

REMEMBER: A paragraph is a group of sentences or 'chunk' of text that describes one stage in a piece of writing.

17 Commas

"When I take a breath, I put a comma."

Many children put full stops when they take a breath too. This means that it can be a tricky way of working out when to put commas or full stops.

There are many reasons for using commas in sentences.

Commas are used to:

- ✓ separate clauses in a sentence:
  Arif sat quietly, as he had been chosen to direct the play, and was watching his friends go through it.
- ✓ separate items in a short list:
  There were crisps, biscuit crumbs, empty wrappers and sticky glasses on the table in front of him.
- ✓ separate dialogue (talking) from narrative (the storyline): *"We keep forgetting our words," giggled Sasha and Aidan.*
  "Come on," Arif said, "you're not really trying."
- ✓ separate terms of address from the rest of the sentence:
  A little later he called out, "Sasha, that was much better. Hey, everyone, how about practising that again?"

HAVE A GO

You can see how important commas are in making the meaning of sentences clear, by reading the rest of the story about Arif and his friends. There are 13 missing commas in the text. Put them in the correct places.

Arif pleased with the progress they were making decided to call for a break. "Let's grab a bite from the kitchen" he suggested "and then if you like we can go out for some fresh air exercise and a change of scene."

The others agreed and Aidan suddenly remembering he had promised to phone his mother made a quick phone call. "It's going really well Mum" he said. "Tell Dad Giles Uncle Jamie and Ellie to be ready for six o'clock."

Never end a sentence with a comma!

Notice how commas have a much more important job than simply saying, 'Take a breath now'. Certainly, when you feel the need to take a breath, there should probably be some kind of punctuation, but not necessarily a comma. Try to use commas in your own writing to make what you want to say clear and avoid **ambiguity**.

18 Other common punctuation marks

"I often forget to put question marks."

"I put exclamation marks all over the place."

"I don't understand how to use all the other marks."

Apart from full stops and commas, there are a number of other common punctuation marks. Here they are:

! ? … ; : ' ' " " - – ( )

Some of them are found at the end of sentences; others are written inside sentences.

How many do you use already? Read the summary of any punctuation marks you are not sure how or when to use.

Finishing sentences

You know that full stops finish sentences (statements). There are three other forms of punctuation that can finish a sentence:

! Exclamation marks help to show emphasis or emotion (such as excitement, surprise or anger). They are used to finish:

- ✓ **an order or command**: *Stop! Wait! Be careful!*
- ✓ **an exclamation**: *What a big cake! How exciting!*

LEARN: Be sparing and only use one ! at a time. Otherwise your writing can become 'over the top'.

? Question marks finish:

- ✓ **a sentence that asks a question**: *Can you help? What's his name?*

… An ellipsis allows a sentence to trail off and creates suspense, so this mark finishes:

- ✓ **any sentence that leaves the reader guessing**: *It didn't take her long to notice …*

Inside sentences

You have seen how commas have different roles in sentences. There are several other punctuation marks that each have their own job. You need to be able to recognise these marks and use them in your writing.

; Semicolons show longer pauses in sentences. They are used:

- ✓ **in long or complex lists that already use commas**: *Lee went off to fetch two parasols, one red and one white; a jug of water with ice; a set of playing cards, and a volleyball, for playing games; towels for lying on; and ice creams all round.*
- ✓ **to link two or more related sentences instead of full stops or conjunctions**: *It was hot; the sun was beating down; we were all bathed in sweat.*

: Colons introduce different elements such as:

- ✓ **a list**: *The recipe needed: two eggs; 250 g flour; a pinch of salt; 500 ml milk.*
- ✓ **an explanation**: *I have two pet hates: spiders and mosquitoes.*
- ✓ **a quotation**: *The note said: "Come at 2 p.m. Bring your bike."*

: Colons introduce different elements such as:

- ✔ a list:
  The recipe needed: two eggs; 250 g flour; a pinch of salt; 500 ml milk.
- ✔ an explanation: *I have two pet hates: spiders and mosquitoes.*
- ✔ a quotation: *The note said: "Come at 2 p.m. Bring your bike."*

An ellipsis allows a sentence to trail off and creates suspense, so this mark introduces:

- ✔ a hesitation or trailing off … and then continuing:
  "Umm … I don't know the answer."

' **Apostrophes** have two very different jobs. They:

- ✔ replace missing letters in **contractions**:
  we would = we'd; he cannot = he can't; Tom is sad = Tom's sad
- ✔ show belonging (possession):
  the fur belonging to the cat = the cat's fur; the room belonging to Sushi = Sushi's room; the bikes belonging to the boys = the boys' bikes.

(Notice how if something belongs to more than one person or thing, the apostrophe goes *after* the **plural noun**.)

> **LEARN:** 'It's' always means either 'it is' or 'it has'. Don't add an apostrophe to 'its' to show possession, just as you would not for *his*, *her* or *our*.

> **LEARN:** Never use apostrophes to make plurals! (See page 93.) Look closely at where you put an apostrophe for singular or plural nouns.

' ' or " " **Inverted commas** are used when **dialogue** is written. They come:

- ✔ before and after the words that are actually spoken but are placed after any punctuation:
  "Come here," called Akshay, "and I'll tell you the secret."

Grammar and punctuation

- Hyphens have two main jobs. They:

> ✓ join two or more words together to make a new idea:
> father-in-law   part-time
> self-confidence   sixty-three
> non-stick
>
> ✓ split a word at the end of a **syllable** if the whole word will not fit on one line:
> Ella noticed that the air was grow-ing cooler.

Look at these ways in which hyphens can change meanings and avoid ambiguity.

> man eating shark   man-eating shark
> recreation   re-creation
> three year-old cousins   twelve-year-old cousins

– Dashes can be used alone or in pairs.

A single dash:

> ✓ attaches an extra point to a sentence:
> He thought it was his cat under the bed – but was it?

LEARN: Dashes are often used in informal writing and in dialogue.

A pair of dashes:

> ✓ separates non-essential information from the rest of a sentence:
> Our first house – the one in the town centre – had a small garden.

( ) Brackets always come in pairs. They are used to:

> ✓ insert useful (but not essential) details in a sentence, like dashes:
> Our first house (the one in the town centre) had a small garden.
>
> ✓ separate numbers and abbreviations from the rest of a sentence:
> His flight (LHR 7604) went from London Heathrow airport (LHR).

LEARN: Where pairs of dashes, brackets or commas are used to add extra information, this can be called **parenthesis**.

Look out for all kinds of punctuation in your reading and ask yourself, whenever you see a punctuation mark, what it is for. Practise using the punctuation you see as you read in your own writing. Especially look out for how speech is punctuated and the use of inverted commas, commas and paragraphs.

HAVE A GO

a Make up a sentence that uses commas, brackets or dashes to show when something is in parenthesis.

....

b Write a sentence including both uses of apostrophes.

....

c Imagine two or three people telling each other about their holidays and write what they say using direct speech.

....

d Link three short related sentences with semicolons.

....

e Write a short, detailed list about four things in your bedroom using a colon and commas.

....

Go over the rules for using the underlined punctuation marks, and then ask an adult to check your writing and punctuation. Did you get them right? If not, keep practising.

EXAM TIP

When you write in an exam, wherever possible show that you understand and can use a wide range of punctuation marks so that you can impress your reader. Be sure to check the punctuation very carefully once you have completed your writing.

19 Word classes or parts of speech

Words are divided into different groups depending on their use. In 11+ English, you must show that you know the main groups. These are:

- **nouns**
- **verbs**
- **adjectives**
- **adverbs**
- **pronouns**
- **prepositions**
- **conjunctions** or **connectives**
- **determiners.**

First, you need to learn the different job each group does in English grammar.

A brief summary of each of these word groups is given in this section. Read through any that you need to revise.

Nouns

- **Common nouns** are general names of people, animals, places, things and events. For example:

people:	crowd	teacher	police officer
animals:	rabbit	cat	bird
places:	school	garden	supermarket
things:	balloon	air	computer
events:	party	holiday	sports day

- **Proper nouns** are special names (or **titles**) of people, animals, places, things or events. They must start with a capital letter to show they are special. For example:

LEARN: Test for a **noun** by putting 'a' or 'the' in front.

people:	Tom	Mum	Mr Scott
animals:	Dutch rabbit	Siamese cat	Emperor penguin
places:	Birmingham	Spain	Derbyshire
things:	July	Playstation	Rolls Royce
events:	Christmas	Yom Kippur	Diwali

- **Abstract nouns** are names of feelings, concepts, or ideas. For example:

beauty	leadership	love	fear
happiness	curiosity	vacancy	appearance

- **Collective nouns** are names of groups or collections of things. For example:

> a flock of sheep   a board of directors   a swarm of bees   a bunch of flowers

A **noun phrase** has a **head word** (the most important word) that is a noun. You can add extra information to a noun and describe it to make a noun phrase or expanded noun phrase. Here are some examples:

> **LEARN:** Nouns are naming words.
> Most common nouns can be singular or plural.
> Some nouns are always plural, such as scissors.
> All proper nouns start with capital letters.

> A dog   A black dog   A black dog with a waggy tail   My black dog with a waggy tail and floppy ears

See how the head word, 'dog', can be expanded with extra information. Notice that there is no verb, so these are all noun phrases.

HAVE A GO

1 In this list of different nouns, underline the common nouns, put circles round the proper nouns, put boxes round the abstract nouns and brackets round the collective nouns:

a gaggle of geese	Sunday	rattlesnake	football	match	anger
Italy	Easter	a pride of lions	Aunty Sue	orchestra	soup
Sorrow	Mr Jarvis	jelly	chimpanzee	pencils	atmosphere

Verbs

- Verbs can be:

  doing words: *jump*   *swim*   *read*

  being words: *like*   *know*   *am*

LEARN: Verbs are words that tell you what is happening to the subject or noun in a sentence.

Verbs must agree with the singular or plural subject of a sentence. (See Section 20.)

- The name of a verb is called the **infinitive**. It usually has 'to' in front:

    to do   to jump   to swim   to read   to like   to know   to be

- The tense of a verb tells you when something is happening:

    present: Today **I go** to the shops. **I am buying** some bread today.

    past: Yesterday **I went** to the shops and **I bought** some bread.

    future: Tomorrow **I will go** to the shops and **I will buy** some bread.

For both the present and the past, there are four main tenses. Here are examples of each:

Present simple
*I go. They think.
He eats. We jump.*

Past simple
*I went. They thought.
He ate. We jumped.*

Present continuous
*I am going. They are thinking.
He is eating. We are jumping.*

Past continuous
*I was going. They were thinking.
He was eating. We were jumping.*

Present perfect
*I have gone. They have thought.
He has eaten. We have jumped.*

Past perfect
*I had gone. They had thought.
He had eaten. We had jumped.*

Present perfect continuous
*I have been going. They have been thinking.
He has been eating. We have been jumping.*

Past perfect continuous
*I had been going. They had been thinking.
He had been eating. We had been jumping.*

- The verbs 'to have' and 'to be' are special verbs called **auxiliary verbs**. They are sometimes called 'helpers' and are used with other verbs in sentences:

    *I **am** going home.   We **have** lost our cat.   Our neighbours **are** looking for it.*

- **Modal verbs** are verbs that help other verbs. They include:

    must   may   might   can   could   will   would   shall   should

and **negatives**:

mustn't   shouldn't   cannot   couldn't   won't   shan't

- Modal verbs are a useful way to indicate the possibility (or not) of something happening. Look at these examples of how the modal verb can change sentences:

> *I might go out.* (Then again, I might not – I am undecided.)
> *I could go out.* (It's an option.)
> *I would go out.* (I would go out, but … I have an excuse!)
> *I should go out.* (I don't really want to go out, but I feel it is my duty to do so.)
> *I will go out.*   (There is no doubt here as this is definitely happening.)

- Modal verbs can help to make verbs that refer to the future.

> *I will go out.*   *I shall go out.*

- You can also talk about future events using 'going to':

> *I am going to go out.*

This is how you can explain something happening later, tomorrow or in the future.

- The **subjunctive form** of a verb is used when we express things that should or could happen. You can spot the subjunctive form if the form 'to be' changes or if the final 's' at the end of the verb is removed.
People often get the subjunctive form wrong, so look out for how it is used in your reading and listening.
Look at the following examples. The sentences on the left have been rewritten on the right to include the subjunctive form of the verb:

Incorrect	Correct
I wish I was able to suggest it.	*I wish I were able to suggest it.*
If I was in charge for the day...	*If I were in charge for the day*
I suggest he writes to her.	*I suggest he write to her.*
I insist they are removed.	*I insist they be removed.*

You can see that it is easy to understand both incorrect and correct versions of the sentences, but if you are going to use accurate grammar, you need to learn how to use the subjunctive.

Grammar and punctuation

Grammar and punctuation

HAVE A GO

2 Change this sentence to the future:

Zak enjoyed his trip to the zoo because he loves animals.

....

3 Change this passive verb sentence to an active verb sentence:

The bird food was eaten by a squirrel.

....

4 Change this present simple verb sentence to a past perfect tense sentence:

We jump on the trampoline.

....

5 Underline the two infinitives in this sentence.

Every day I try to tidy my room and to prepare my lunchbox for school.

6 Underline the modal verb in this sentence:

Sarah wasn't sure if she should go skating or not.

Adjectives

- Adjectives can describe:

colour:	golden	green	transparent
size:	enormous	medium	tiny
mood:	happy	miserable	uncertain

REMEMBER: Adjectives describe nouns and pronouns.

- Adjectives can also compare things. There are three groups of comparing adjectives:

    simple: *A hedgehog is small.* (No ending is added to the adjective.)

    comparative: *A mouse is smaller.* (–er is added to the adjective.)

    superlative: *An ant is the smallest.* (–est is added to the adjective.)

The endings –er and –est are usually added to adjectives with one-syllable or adjectives with two syllables that end in –y. The words *more* or *most* are written before adjectives with two or more syllables instead of these endings, for example:

This book is more *helpful.*   *This is the* most *popular book.*

- **Adjectival phrases** modify or change a noun. They add extra information to the noun in a sentence.

- Here, the noun is *lemon*. The adjectival phrases are in colour.
  The lemon was sour. *The lemon was* incredibly sour. *The lemon* from the bowl *was* incredibly sour.

Adverbs

- Adverbs describe how, when, where and how often something happens:

How:	*He ran* slowly.	*She read* quietly.
When:	*They arrived* early.	*The shop opened* late.
Where:	*The boys played football* outside.	*She walked* upstairs.
How often:	*I practise my trumpet* regularly.	*You* often *go to visit her.*

REMEMBER: Adverbs usually describe verbs. Adverbs often end in –ly.

- An **adverbial phrase** is a group of two or more words that adds extra detail to a verb. Adverbial phrases can be to do with time but also place (where), manner (how) and frequency (how often). If more than one is used, they go in that order. Here the verb is 'ate'. The adverbial phrases are underlined.

> *She ate her pudding. She ate her pudding* <u>as slowly as possible</u>. *She ate her pudding* <u>with huge enjoyment</u>.
> *She ate her pudding* <u>yesterday</u> <u>out in the garden</u>, <u>little by little</u>, <u>occasionally grinning happily</u>.
>   time   place   manner   frequency

- **Fronted adverbials** are adverbs or adverbial phrases that are placed at the front of the sentence for effect. A fronted adverbial is usually followed by a comma. Look at these sentences with the adverb moved to the front of the sentence:

> *She ran quickly to the park.*   Quickly, *she ran to the park.*
> *The boys played football outside.*   Outside, *the boys played football.*
> *I practise my trumpet every evening.*   Every evening, *I practise my trumpet.*

- **Time adverbials** are used to structure order in texts. The time adverbials include 'first', 'next', 'then', 'finally', 'now', 'often', 'later', 'daily', 'monthly' and 'yearly'. Here are some examples of time adverbials used in sentences:

> I can meet you *later*.   We are on our way *now*.   Who is coming *next*?

Time adverbials may not always be at the end or in the middle of a sentence. They can also be placed at the beginning to make a fronted adverbial:

> *First*, I want to write about my friends. *Next*, I'll discuss my pets. *Finally*, I will describe my home.

HAVE A GO

7 Read each sentence. Underline the adjectives. Put a circle round the adverbs. Put a box round the fronted adverbials.

a   Yesterday evening, I was really surprised to see a flock of large, white doves settle on the next-door roof.

b   Every day is different when we walk to school because they are building new houses along the main road.

c   Flip, Misha's huge black Labrador, was frantically chasing a fluffy tabby cat round the garden, barking madly.

d   After a lot of effort, Kubi managed to complete his enormous, complicated jigsaw puzzle.

e   Bring along warm clothes, a packed lunch, a small notepad and two sharp pencils.

Pronouns

Pronouns stand in for a noun so that you don't need to repeat the noun again and again. There are two groups of pronouns that replace common and **proper nouns** in particular ways: **personal** and **possessive pronouns**.

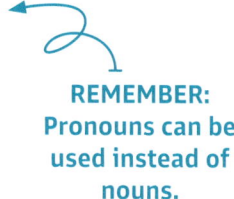

REMEMBER: Pronouns can be used instead of nouns.

- Personal pronouns can be singular or plural:

Olivia left for school at 7.30 a.m.	→	*She* left for school at 7.30 a.m.
Logan and Amruta worked on *the project* together.	→	*They* worked on *it* together.
Harry and I went to see *Matthew and Evie*.	→	*We* went to see *them*.
Has *Theo* seen *the film*?	→	Has *he* seen *it*?

- Possessive pronouns tell us who or what owns or has something:

That bike belongs to *Kang*.	→	That bike is *his*. It's *his*.
This book belongs to *me*.	→	This book is *mine*.
The new car belongs to *Jo and Kim*.	→	The new car is *theirs*. It's *theirs*.
The house belongs to *us*.	→	The house is *ours*.
The cat has a red collar.	→	*Its* collar is red.

HAVE A GO

8 Rewrite each sentence using pronouns.

  a Ori and Matt loved playing Minecraft.

  ....

  b The coat belongs to me.

  ....

  c Lisa enjoyed the play.

  ....

  d My brother and I visited our grandparents.

  ....

> **LEARN:** The **possessive pronoun** 'its' means belonging to it.
>
> The short form 'it's' only ever stands for 'it is' or 'it has'.

EXAM TIP

Be very careful when you use pronouns in your writing.

It needs to be clear what or who the pronoun stands for, otherwise you may confuse your readers.

There are two other kinds of pronouns that are often used in sentences:

- **Relative pronouns** introduce information about a noun or a pronoun. They include words like 'which', 'where', 'when', 'who', 'whose' or 'that'. You can connect a main clause to a subordinate clause or noun phrase using a relative pronoun to make a **relative clause**. Here are some examples. The relative clause is underlined:

> I don't like the cat <u>**which** catches the baby birds</u>.
> The beautiful village, <u>**where** Kirsty lives with her sister</u>, is quite far away.
> He doesn't like summer <u>**when** it is too hot</u>.
> My disabled brother, <u>**who** works at the shop</u>, loves his job there.
> She is the woman <u>**whose** car was damaged</u>.
> The special card for Daisy's tenth birthday <u>**that** I posted last week</u> has still not arrived.

- **Indefinite pronouns** refer generally to people or things:

Tell me all that you know.	Tell me **everything**.
Tell me a thing you know.	Tell me **something**.
Tell me one thing or other you know.	Tell me **anything**. Tell me **nothing**.
Show me all the people there.	Show me **everyone**.
Show me one person there.	Show me **someone**.
Show me one person or another there.	Show me **anyone**. Show me **no one**.

HAVE A GO

9 Complete each sentence with a relative clause using the relative pronoun that is given.

a Our old car, which ...., needs new tyres.

b The children prefer breaktimes when ....

c My friend Amy, who lives ...., is coming over today.

d We love going to the park, where ....

e Jamie's dog, whose ...., loves chewing things.

Discuss your answers with an adult for feedback.

Prepositions

- Prepositions link nouns and pronouns to other parts of a sentence. They show:

LEARN: 'Pre-' means 'before' or 'in front of'. A preposition is written before or in front of a noun.

position:	*in* the room	*behind* the house	*near* the school
direction:	*up* the stairs	*through* the window	*over* the fence
time:	*during* break	*before* assembly	*on* Saturday

HAVE A GO

10 Underline the prepositions in this sentence. There are 12 to find!

During the Fun Run in the country park at the weekend, we had to go through mud, over fences, under hedges, up a hill, down a water slide and across a swampy field, getting to the end before lunch at 1 p.m.

Conjunctions

Conjunctions (or connectives) are words that are used to join (or connect) two or more clauses, words or phrases.

A *junction* is a join, so you can recognise con*junction*s because they join.

You need to learn two kinds of conjunctions: **coordinating conjunctions** and **subordinating conjunctions**.

- There are seven main coordinating conjunctions in English: for, and, nor, but, or, yet, so. These are used to connect two or more words or clauses that are equally important.
- The **mnemonic** FANBOYS can help remind you of them. Here are examples using these coordinating conjunctions:

> We took umbrellas *for* it was raining.
> I had lunch *and* went for a walk.
> Mo didn't like maths, *nor* going swimming.
> Saji loved pizza *but* preferred pasta.
> Would you like a banana *or* grapes?
> The weather is cold *yet* bright.
> Olly was tired *so* found it hard to concentrate.

Notice that you can often leave out the subject after the conjunction.

- Subordinating conjunctions are used to join a main clause with a subordinate (or less important) clause. They often show cause and effect.
There are ten main ones in English:

> *if, since, as, when, although, while, after, before, until, because*

- The mnemonic I SAW A WABUB (whatever that is!) can help remind you of them.
- Here are some examples of using some of the most common subordinating conjunctions.

> I couldn't do my homework *because* it was too hard.
> Jack will miss the train *if* he doesn't hurry up.
> Alex wants to work at her tennis skills *until* she has improved.
> The squirrel was hiding nuts *before* the cold weather set in.

- Notice how you could switch the two clauses round, for example:

Before the cold weather set in, the squirrel was hiding nuts.

HAVE A GO

11 Try using each of the different conjunctions in sentences of your own.

12 Underline the conjunctions in these sentences:

  a It was pouring with rain after the match was over.

  b Although she had forgotten her books, Eva didn't get told off.

  c Our cat was really ill last week but she has recovered now.

  Show them to an adult for feedback.

13 Try switching the first two sentences (2a and 2b) so that the subordinating conjunction is at the beginning. Which version do you like best?

Determiners

A determiner is a word that goes before a noun. There are several types of determiners. Here are the types of determiners with some examples.

REMEMBER: Conjunctions *join* clauses or sentences together to make more complex sentences.

Articles	Demonstratives	Numbers	Ordinals	Possessives	Quantifiers
a	that	fifty-two	first	her	all
an	these	four	last	his	every
the	this	one hundred	next	my	more
	those	six	sixtieth	their	none
		twenty	third	your	some

- You use 'a' before any word that begins with a **consonant**, for example *a ball, a taxi, a girl*.
- You use 'an' before any word that begins with a **vowel**, for example *an action, an elephant, an owl*, unless the vowel is pronounced like a consonant, for example *a one-day event*.
- You use 'an' before any word that sounds as though it begins with a vowel even if the letter is actually a consonant, usually 'h', for example *an hour, an honour, an heir*, but *a hospital, a hotel*.

Once you understand these main **word classes** or **parts of speech**, you need to be able to spot them in your reading and use them in your writing.

HAVE A GO

14 Put the letters a–j from the left list next to the words they go with in the right list, or join pairs with a line.

a	determiner	Manchester
b	abstract noun	should
c	preposition	we
d	subordinating conjunction	larger
e	adverbial	every
f	comparative adjective	so
g	pronoun	luckily
h	modal verb	friendship
i	coordinating conjunction	into
j	proper noun	while

20 Subjects and objects

"These words sound the same to me!"

Yes, many people find them a little confusing. Working through this section should help to make them clearer.

Most complete statements and questions have a subject and a verb. Orders and exclamations often leave out one or both of these:

"Come!" "Wait there." "No!"

The subject of a sentence tells you who or what the sentence is about. The verb tells you what is happening. The object tells you what is affected by the verb. The subject is usually a common or proper noun or a noun phrase (a group of words including a noun). Remember:

> ✔ a noun can be replaced by a pronoun
> ✔ a subject can be singular or plural
> ✔ a verb must agree with its subject.

Look at these examples:

Chang looked in the shed.

Chang is doing the action in this sentence, so **Chang**, a **singular proper noun**, is the subject.

The bikes were gone.

The bikes, a **plural common noun**, are the subject in this sentence and the verb agrees with them.

Poor Chang looked in the shed.

In this sentence, the **noun phrase**, **Poor Chang**, is the subject.

He wanted to fetch the mountain bikes. They were gone.

The subjects are **pronouns**: **He** and **They**.

> **LEARN:** The subject of a clause or sentence is what or who it is about. The object of a clause or sentence is what or who is affected by the action of the subject and the verb.

Grammar and punctuation

Often, a sentence has an object. An object is affected in some way by the action of the subject and the verb.

Look again at this sentence:

Chang looked in the shed.

Chang is the subject.

looked is the verb.

the shed is the object affected by the subject and the verb.

Look at this sentence:

He wanted to fetch the bikes.

He is the subject.

wanted to fetch is the verb.

the bikes is the object.

HAVE A GO

1 In each of the following sentences, underline the subjects, put boxes round the objects and circle the verbs. Then change the subjects and objects to *pronouns* and write the new sentences on the lines.

   a The bird hopped among the branches.

   ....

   b Susie and I collected conkers.

   ....

   c Our hockey team won the match.

   ....

2 Add objects to these sentences:

   a The boy climbed ....

   b Our dog was eating ....

   c None of the children wanted to bring ....

3 Write a suitable <u>subject</u> and a <u>verb</u> to complete these sentences.

a .... under the hedge.

b .... some flowers in the meadow.

c .... ten sums on the board.

Show your answers to an adult for feedback.

21 Gender and diminutives

"I find these words quite hard to remember."

They can look rather off-putting, but they will come in very useful once you understand them.

In 11+ English you may need to show that you know the **gender** of nouns: whether they are **masculine** or **feminine**.

LEARN:
Masculine means male; feminine means female.

Many nouns have different words for male and female kinds. Sometimes the suffix '–ess' is added to a male word to make the female version. Look at these examples:

Masculine	Feminine	Masculine	Feminine
hero	heroine	father	mother
prince	princess	count	countess
lord	lady	gander	goose
nephew	niece	fox	vixen

You also need to know the **diminutive** forms of some nouns for 11+ English.

In the case of animals, diminutives mean their babies or young.

In the case of objects, diminutives mean smaller versions of them.

Some diminutives are formed by adding a **prefix** or a **suffix** to a **root word**. (See pages 101–103.)

REMEMBER:
Diminutive means a smaller version of something.

Look at the examples below.

Larger form	Diminutive form	Larger form	Diminutive form
bus	minibus	goose	gosling
book	booklet	pig	piglet
kitchen	kitchenette	computer	microcomputer

Diminutives can be used as nicknames for first names. For instance, *Nicholas* is often shortened to *Nick* or *Nicky*. Here are some more examples:

Full first name	Diminutive form	Full first name	Diminutive form
Christina	Chris, Tina	Matthew	Matt
Victor	Vic, Tori	Rajesh	Raj
Elizabeth	Liz, Beth	Rebecca	Becky, Becca
Agata	Aga	Rashida	Rashi

HAVE A GO

Collect as many words as you can in your notebook where the masculine noun is different from the feminine noun. This particularly applies to jobs, animals and family members. If there is one, add the diminutive form as well.

Here are some to get you started:

goose   fox   niece   waiter   cow   uncle   host   bride   pig

22 Synonyms and antonyms

"I get a bit muddled with these."

You may need to show that you know what these words mean in 11+ English.

Using synonyms in your writing helps to avoid repetition and can make your writing more interesting.

LEARN:
Synonyms are *similar*.
Antonyms are *opposite*.

- Synonyms are words that have the same or similar meanings. For instance, here are some synonyms for the word 'big':

grand   large   sizeable   huge   bulky   significant   substantial

- Antonyms are words that have opposite meanings. For instance, here are some antonyms for the word 'big':

> little   small   minute   tiny   skinny   insignificant   miniature

(See Develop your vocabulary on page 33.)

Always think about meanings before using synonyms and antonyms. In English, we have many words with dozens of different meanings. If you look up words like 'mark' or 'catch' or 'play' in a dictionary, you will find numbers showing several examples of the same word, explaining the different meanings.

REMEMBER: A thesaurus is a good source of synonyms and antonyms.

LEARN: Not all words have opposites – there are no antonyms for the word 'green', for example.

The words you choose must always fit the **context** (meaning) of a sentence. You may also need to think about word classes. (See page 60.)

Look at these examples:

*The parcel felt very **light**.*

There are many synonyms for the word 'light', for example 'glow', 'weightless', 'insubstantial', 'ignite', 'delicate', 'soft', 'pale', 'elegant', 'bright'.

All of these have different meanings and you need to understand the context of the sentence before choosing a synonym. In this example, 'light' means 'not heavy', so **insubstantial** would be a good synonym to use here.

*The colour of my walls is **light** blue.*

There are also many antonyms for the word 'light', for example 'dark', 'gloomy', 'shade', 'heavy', 'serious', 'sinister', 'extinguish'.

You can't choose the most appropriate antonym if you haven't understood the meaning of 'light' in the sentence. In this sentence, 'light' means 'pale', so **dark** would be a suitable antonym.

*I switched on the **light**.*

In this example, the word 'light' is a noun, not an adjective. This means suitable synonyms would be 'lamp', 'torch' or 'lantern'. For this meaning, 'light' has no antonym.

Grammar and punctuation

> **HAVE A GO**
>
> 1 Write an antonym for each of these words:
>
>   a over......................
>
>   b timid......................
>
>   c rough......................
>
>   d late......................
>
>   e beginning......................
>
> 2 Write a synonym for each of these words:
>
>   a exhausted......................
>
>   b easy......................
>
>   c smiled......................
>
>   d create......................
>
>   e wrong......................

23 Abbreviations and acronyms

"There are hundreds!"

Yes, there are, but no one expects you to know them all! Many individual words and groups of words are often shortened when used in speech or writing. You should make sure you are familiar with some of the most common abbreviations and that you can recognise some useful acronyms.

Here are some common abbreviations, which use part of the original word:

Abbreviation	Full word
bike	bicycle
fridge	refrigerator
photo	photograph
phone	telephone
rhino	rhinoceros

Did you know that all of the words in the left-hand column were abbreviations?

Abbreviations can also be formed from the first letters (initials) of the words being shortened. For example:

Abbreviation	Full phrase
BBC	**B**ritish **B**roadcasting **C**orporation
HGV	**h**eavy **g**oods **v**ehicle
PC	**p**ersonal **c**omputer or **p**olice **c**onstable
RSPB	**R**oyal **S**ociety for the **P**rotection of **B**irds

Notice how each initial letter is pronounced in these abbreviations.

Some other commonly used abbreviations come from **Latin**. For these you will need to understand what the phrase means rather than learn the Latin words they stand for. The examples below are often used in writing:

Abbreviation	Full meaning
a.m.	before noon
e.g.	for example
etc.	and so on
PS	written afterwards
v.	against

REMEMBER: Abbreviations are shortened versions of words.

An **acronym** is a form of abbreviation that is usually made up of the initial letters of the group of words being shortened. Acronyms are different to the abbreviations listed in the second table above, as they are pronounced as single words.

Here are some acronyms you may recognise:

Acronym	Full phrase
FIFA	**F**édération **I**nternationale de **F**ootball **A**ssociation
laser	**l**ight **a**mplification by **s**timulated **e**mission of **r**adiation
NATO	**N**orth **A**tlantic **T**reaty **O**rganization
Ofsted	**O**ffice **f**or **St**andards in **E**ducation
RAM	**r**andom-**a**ccess **m**emory

Grammar and punctuation

HAVE A GO

Make a collection of abbreviations and acronyms as you come across them and write them in your notebook. Here are some to start you off:

Abbreviations:
HQ   bus   GMT   pub   ASAP   NHS   p.m.

Acronyms:
The Beeb   PIN   co-ed   Wi-Fi

24 Compound words

"I'm not quite sure what they are."

Many people find compound words puzzling.

Compound words are made by joining two or three smaller words together to make a longer one.

Here are two examples of compound words:

REMEMBER:
A compound word usually has a different meaning from the individual words that make it.

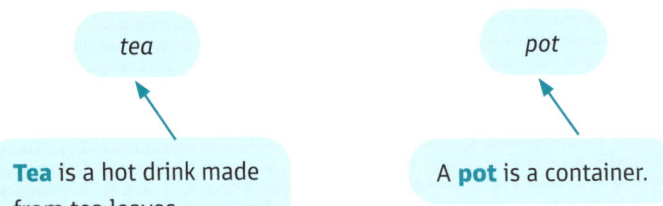

Tea is a hot drink made from tea leaves.

A **pot** is a container.

Put together, the two words make a new idea: **teapot** (a covered pot with a spout in which tea is brewed).

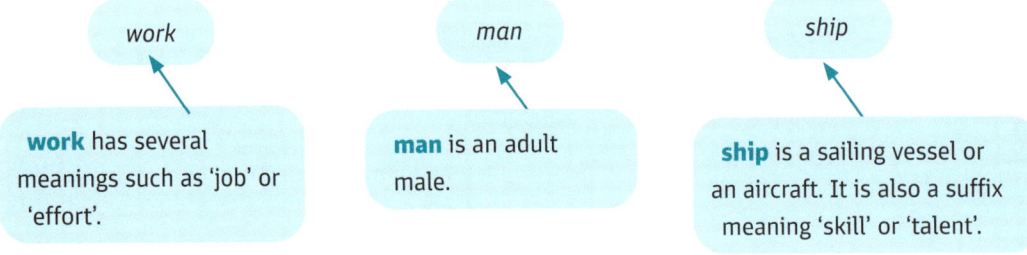

work has several meanings such as 'job' or 'effort'.

man is an adult male.

ship is a sailing vessel or an aircraft. It is also a suffix meaning 'skill' or 'talent'.

Put together, the three words make a new idea: **workmanship** (the talent of a skilled manual worker).

HAVE A GO

Make as many compound words as you can by putting these words together in different ways:

over   ball   coat   foot   waist   snow   arm   line   under

Collect more as you spot them and write them in your notebook.

25 Direct and reported speech

"I find changing from one to the other tricky."

It can be quite difficult; there is a lot to think about.

There are two ways of writing speech that you need to be familiar with.

- Direct speech uses the words that are actually spoken, for instance:
  Jarek called, *"Help me! I'm drowning!"*
- Reported speech explains what was said but does not use the exact words. You can write the same thing as if you are reporting something. So, in reported speech, the above example could be written as:
  Jarek called for help because he thought he was drowning.
  Notice especially how the tense changes between direct and reported speech.
- In the first example, Jarek's words are written in the present tense.
- When his words are written as reported speech, the sentence is written in the past tense. This is quite tricky and you need to practise changing one to the other. Look out for both kinds of speech in your reading.

REMEMBER: When writing direct speech, pay close attention to all the punctuation needed.

HAVE A GO

1 Rewrite these direct speech sentences as reported speech.

   a "I'd like a party on my birthday, Mum," said Dan.

      ....

   b Mr Slater remarked, "It feels like winter today."

      ....

c "Come inside, Charlie," said Grandad, "and have a hot drink with us."

   ....

2 Now rewrite these reported speech sentences as direct speech.

   a The principal told the children that their behaviour was improving.

      ....

   b My father complained that he was feeling tired.

      ....

   c Rosie's mother asked if she had remembered the note from school.

      ....

26 Avoiding common errors: what NOT to do!

There are some common grammar traps that people often fall into. If you know about them, you can try to avoid them. Here are some of the main ones:

Double negatives

If you use two negative words in a phrase or sentence, this is called a **double negative**. Here are some examples:

> We **don't** have **no** money.
> There **weren't no** raisins left in the jar.

If you really think about them, the two negatives cancel each other out, so the sentences actually mean:

> We **do** have money.
> There **were** raisins left in the jar.

To avoid this problem, you have to use the words *any* or *no*. For instance, the first example of double negatives could be correctly written as:

*We don't have **any** money.*   or   *We have **no** money.*

How should the second example be written?

When you are writing dialogue, though, it can be amusing to use double negatives now and again; people often use them when they're talking. Listen for examples of this or find examples in dialogue in your reading.

'Of' or 'have'?

*We should **have** gone, since they could **have** taken us.*

In the sentence above, notice the use of 'have'.

When you say the sentence aloud, you will notice that the word 'have' gets swallowed up and sounds more like 'of'. You must never write 'of' if you want to use correct grammar.

If you want to 'swallow' the 'have' to make it sound more like 'of', then use contractions in your writing. Using contractions, the example above would be written:

*We should**'ve** gone, since they could**'ve** taken us.*

How often do you write 'of' instead of 'have'? Look out for this error in your own writing!

**REMEMBER:
Contractions are often used in dialogue.**

Past tenses

These can cause problems because there are many **irregular** forms that do not follow familiar patterns. Listen to a three-year-old talking and you will hear some mistakes that crop up in older children's writing too!

"I hurted my knee and it bleeded so I did cry."

The three-year-old has not yet learned to say:

"I hurt my knee and it bled so I cried."

You need to learn **irregular past tenses** as you come across them. Here are some common **irregular tenses** that you should be familiar with:

Infinitive	Present tense	Past tense
to buy	I buy	I bought
to catch	you catch	you caught
to eat	he eats	he ate

Infinitive	Present tense	Past tense
to keep	she keeps	she kept
to make	it makes	it made
to run	we run	we ran
to speak	they speak	they spoke
to swim	they swim	they swam

Sometimes when English is spoken, people will use different forms of the **past tense**. There is nothing wrong with these, but there are standard forms that you should know for 11+ English.

For instance, many people will say:

"I *done* my homework last night."

You need to know that in **Standard English** the correct way to say and write this is:

"I *did* my homework last night."

'I' or 'me'?

Many people find deciding on whether to use 'I' or 'me' in a piece of writing challenging.

Look at these examples of children's writing:

Me and my brother went out to play football.

Su Lin and me handed in our homework on time.

When people are talking, they often make mistakes in these kinds of sentences. When you are writing, however, you need to show that you know whether to use 'I' or 'me'.

'I' must be used when you are the subject or one of the subjects of the sentence. (See page 73.) In the two sentences above, it would be clearly wrong to say, *Me went out to play football* or *Me handed in my homework on time*, because you are the subject.

If you are doing something with someone else, then the other person's name comes first. That's only polite!

The correct versions of the two sentences are:

My brother and I went out to play football.

Su Lin and I handed in our homework on time.

My aunt sent the parcel to you and I.

Dad told Oscar and I to wait for him.

'Me' must be used when you are the object of the sentence. If you split the sentences up into two, it makes it easier to see what is happening.

*My aunt sent it to you. My aunt sent it to **me**.*
*Dad told Oscar to wait for him. Dad told **me** to wait for him.*

The correct versions of these two sentences should be:

*My aunt sent it to **you and me**.*
*Dad told **Oscar and me** to wait for him.*

'Better' or 'best', 'worse' or 'worst', 'fewer' or 'less'?

These forms of adjectives can cause many people problems. You have to make sure that you use the correct form of the adjective when you are comparing.

These sentences are incorrect:	These sentences are correct:
This jacket is the best of the two.	*This jacket is **the better of** the two.*
Sula is the worse chatterbox in the class.	*Sula is the **worst** chatterbox in the class.*
Ava made less mistakes than Rory.	*Ava made **fewer** mistakes than Rory.*

*This jacket is **the better of** the two.* You are comparing two jackets, so that is why you need the **comparative** form 'better' rather than 'best'.

*Sula is the **worst** chatterbox in the class.* You need to use the **superlative adjective**, not the **comparative adjective** for describing Sula because there are more than two people in her class.

*Ava made **fewer** mistakes than Rory.* Use 'fewer' rather than 'less' to compare the number of mistakes made by Ava and Rory.

You use 'less' for amounts of something but 'fewer' for numbers of things, so:

*There's **less** water in your bottle than in Lily's.*

*There are **fewer** bottles in the fridge today than there were yesterday.*

(See page 64 for more details on how to form comparative and superlative adjectives.)

Look out for these adjective uses in your reading and try to use them correctly.

Spelling

In 11+ English you need to show that your spelling is as accurate as you can make it. It is important that you are careful and try to spell so that what you have to say can be understood by someone else.

The English language can be quite challenging to spell. That is because it has developed from many different languages combined over the centuries. Spellings only became fixed when dictionaries were first printed. Some people seem to be very good at spelling. They tend to be wide and attentive readers who are interested in words. Many people struggle. The words just won't stick.

"I'm awful at spelling."

27 Improving your spelling

You will probably have had spellings to learn every week at school, so by Year 5 there will be many words that you can spell. No one is expecting you to be able to spell every word you write perfectly, but you do need to spell well enough to communicate in 11+ English.

- When spelling, you need to know that all English words are made from 26 letters in the alphabet. There are **vowels** and **consonants**. The vowels are *a, e, i, o, u* and sometimes *y*. Your voice can make the sounds of vowels using air from your breath through your vocal chords. The other letters are called consonants and are formed by using lips, tongue or throat to stop your breath moving. The letter *y* can be a consonant in words like 'your' or a vowel in words like 'my' or 'happy'.
- You need to know the names of the vowels as they are in the alphabet, which are the *long* vowel sounds but also the *short* vowel sounds: 'a' (as in *apple*), 'e' (as in *elephant*), 'i' (as in *imp*), 'o' (as in *orange*), 'u' (as in *umbrella*).
- A word may have one **syllable** or more than one. A syllable must contain at least one vowel and will make one sound. You can say the syllables separately or clap them.
- When two letters make one sound, like 'ai', 'ee', 'oi' and so on, it is called a **digraph**. (See page 92 for split digraphs.)
- When three letters make one sound, like 'igh', 'ore', 'ear' and so on, it is called a **trigraph**.

EXAM TIP

Showing your ability to spell well is part of an English 11+ exam. Many people find spelling very hard. Always try to sound out words you want to use in syllables, and make sure you write what you want to say, even if the spellings may not be quite right. That way you will be able to communicate and show your extensive **vocabulary**. Really learn the **exceptions** to the spelling rules in this section.

REMEMBER: Almost all rules have exceptions!

Here are the most important things you can do to improve your spelling:

- ✓ Be aware of the most common spelling errors. (See Learning awkward spellings on page 88).
- ✓ Learn the most important spelling rules, such as:
  - *'i' before 'e' except after 'c' if it sounds like 'eee';*
  - *When two vowels go a-walking, the first vowel does the talking.*
- ✓ Practise spellings using the method 'look, say in syllables, cover, write, check'.
- ✓ Set yourself challenges: choose ten new useful words a week to learn using a spelling list.
- ✓ Sound out words in syllables; make up rhymes; march to them or clap them. Spot syllables that are **stressed** and **unstressed**.
- ✓ When learning a new word, ask yourself these questions:
  - Is it made up of familiar smaller words?
  - Does it have a common **letter string**?
  - Is it based on a common **root word**?
  - Does it have a **prefix** or **suffix** you recognise?
- ✓ Group words in your mind and on paper, according to their letter patterns, for example '–ight', '–ur', '–ous', '–tion'.
- ✓ Spot and learn **silent letters** in words like *i*s*land*, *crumb*, *k*nock or *s*word.
- ✓ Try to make up **mnemonics** to help remember difficult words, for example *b*ig *e*lephants *c*an *a*lways *u*nderstand *s*mall *e*lephants for spelling 'because'.
- ✓ Get into the habit of using a dictionary, thesaurus or spellchecker to make sure that you have the right meaning and the right spelling.
- ✓ Practise spellings by enjoying word searches, crossword puzzles and word games.
- ✓ Be interested in words and their spellings. Collect spellings of words you find tricky, but like and want to use.

28 Learning awkward spellings

These are some of the most awkward sets of spellings you need to be aware of for 11+ English:

- **homophones**
- doubling letters
- one letter misplaced
- frequent culprits
- magic 'e'
- **singulars** and **plurals**
- common letter strings
- **homonyms**
- adding prefixes
- adding suffixes
- **silent letters**
- –shun suffixes
- unstressed vowels

There is a section here on each of these with special hints and ideas for practice.

Exceptions are especially difficult and need to be learned separately. Look out for the Learn boxes to help you with these.

Look through all the sections that you are unsure about or need to brush up on.

Homophones

Homophones are words that *sound* exactly the same but are spelled differently and have different meanings. There are hundreds of homophones. They come in pairs and sometimes in groups of three or even four.

Here are some of the homophones that come up all the time and can cause confusion. People find them particularly tricky to spell because you have to be able to tell the difference between their meanings and spellings.

LEARN: 'Homo' means *same*; 'phone' means *sound*.

air/heir	*affect/effect*	*aloud/allowed*	*are/our*
be/bee	*beech/beach*	*board/bored*	*by/buy/bye*
caught/court	*course/coarse*	*current/currant*	*for/four*
flower/flour	*great/grate*	*guest/guessed*	*hair/hare*
heard/herd	*hole/whole*	*its/it's*	*key/quay*
led/lead	*main/mane*	*new/knew*	*not/knot*
no/know	*our/hour*	*pale/pail*	*past/passed*
practise/practice	*pray/prey*	*principal/principle*	*rain/reign/rein*

right/write/rite/wright   road/rode/rowed   route/root   saw/sore
seen/scene   serial/cereal   so/sew/sow   stationery/stationary
steal/steel   sun/son   their/there/they're   through/threw
thrown/throne   tide/tied   to/two/too   waist/waste
way/weigh   week/weak   where/wear   which/witch
whine/wine   who's/whose   would/wood   you/ewe/yew
you're/your

Spelling

Pay special attention to learning homophones, both to their spellings and their meanings. It can help to:

✓ draw pictures next to the ones you find especially confusing

✓ make up reminders like: 'stationery' has the letter 'e' for 'envelope' in it.

Also look out for awkward homophones where one of the pair or group is spelled with an **apostrophe**.

Be really careful about using these correctly!

HAVE A GO

1 In this passage, underline the correct homophone in each pair of brackets, thinking hard about the meaning each time.

Making (there / their / they're) (weigh / way) (through / threw) the (beach / beech) (would / wood) (which / witch) (lead / led) (to / too / two) the (main / mane) sandy (beach / beech), Ahmed and Jake (new / knew) that they were only (aloud / allowed) (to / too / two) use the (root / route) that (past / passed) the golf (course / coarse) (where / wear) (there / their / they're) dads were having a (practice / practise) game before the (principal / principle) tournament of the season. The low (beach / beech) branches (caught / court) at (there / their / they're) (hair / hare) (so / sew / sow) it took them a (hole / whole) (our / hour) before at last they (saw / sore) the (course / coarse), (waste / waist)-high grass of the dunes with the (sea / see) beyond.

'Nearly (there / their / they're)!' shouted Jake. 'Race (you / ewe / yew), Ahmed!'

'(Your / You're) the winner,' puffed Ahmed, as they reached the sand.

Doubling letters

One of the most common spelling errors is forgetting to double a consonant when you need to keep the vowel sound short. Can you see which 10 words have been spelled incorrectly in this sentence?

Jack was runing to put the rubish in the bin but at the begining of the drive he sudenly spoted a funy chuby rabit sliping out of its burow.

Here are some hints that can help to remind you when to double consonants:

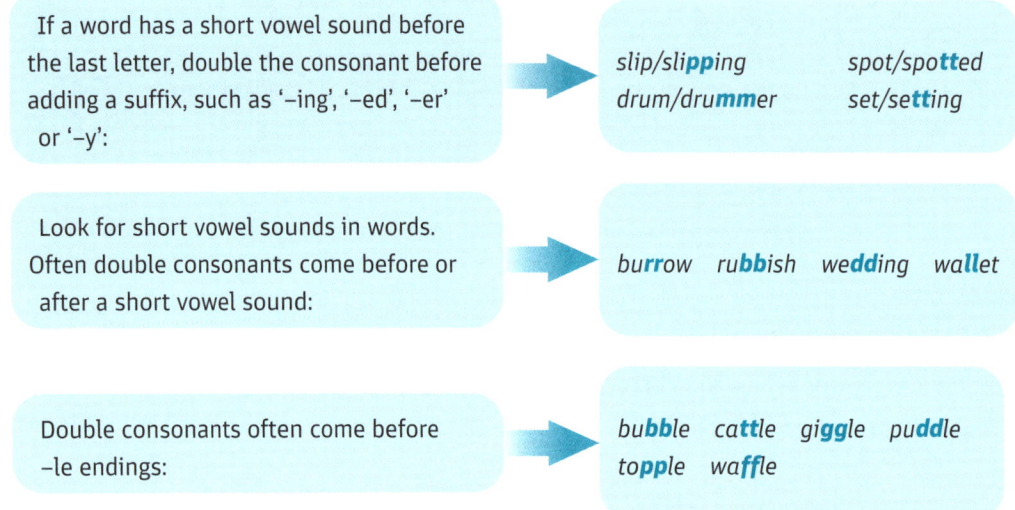

| If a word has a short vowel sound before the last letter, double the consonant before adding a suffix, such as '–ing', '–ed', '–er' or '–y': | ➔ | slip/sli**pp**ing   spot/spo**tt**ed
drum/dru**mm**er   set/se**tt**ing |

| Look for short vowel sounds in words. Often double consonants come before or after a short vowel sound: | ➔ | bu**rr**ow   ru**bb**ish   we**dd**ing   wa**ll**et |

| Double consonants often come before –le endings: | ➔ | bu**bb**le   ca**tt**le   gi**gg**le   pu**dd**le
to**pp**le   wa**ff**le |

Here are some examples of words where both versions with or without the doubled consonant make sense. Look out for pairs of words like these and add to the list if you can.

shinning/shining   planned/planed   sitting/siting   hopping/hoping
pinning/pining   holly/holy   dinner/diner   latter/later
comma/coma   mopping/moping   tapped/taped   matting/mating
lopping/loping   starring/staring   ridding/riding   barring/baring
slopped/sloped   scarred/scared   dessert/desert   bidding/biding

HAVE A GO

2 Choose five of the pairs of words in the example box above. Make up a sentence including each pair to show their meanings.

Here is the first pair made into a sentence:

Kit was <u>shinning</u> up the willow tree with the sun <u>shining</u> in his eyes.

Write the sentences and show them to an adult to discuss meanings.

One letter misplaced

It is amazing how often some word pairs are confused. Misplacing, leaving out or changing just one letter can alter the meaning of a sentence or make it difficult to understand. Read the word pairs below and really study the order of the letters.

Same letters, different order:
from/form   minuet/minute   quiet/quite
split/spilt   trial/trail   untie/unite

One letter more or less:
country/county   exciting/exiting   first/fist   learn/lean   of/off
started/stared   thorough/through   through/though   where/were

One letter different:
pointed/painted   wander/wonder   where/there   effect/affect

Make sure that you check these Eds of words very thoroughly in your writing.

Frequent culprits

There may be words that always seem to let you down. Here are some examples of words that can be frequent culprits:

answer   beautiful   beginning   busy   country
definitely   describe   design   excellent   favourite
February   friend   height   measure   necessary
separate   scene   special   tomorrow   tongue
usual   young

If these (or other words) constantly let you down, try to practise them every day until you know them. Make a poster of them for your room and get your family to test you regularly.

Magic 'e' (split digraph)

Be aware of how the letter 'e' can completely change one word to make another by changing a short vowel sound into a long vowel sound. (See page 86.)

Look at the examples below, which show how magic 'e' works. Say each pair aloud and listen to the difference the magic 'e' makes to the way you pronounce the words.

> bar/bare   cloth/clothe   grim/grime   kit/kite   pin/pine
> quit/quite   rod/rode   scar/scare   scrap/scrape   slid/slide
> spit/spite   star/stare   strip/stripe

When the letter 'e' is at the end of a word, it doesn't always change the sound of the vowel. With many ancient words, such as 'come', 'some', 'gone', and all the words ending in a 'v' sound, such as 'have', 'give', 'love', 'above', 'twelve', the final 'e' doesn't make a long vowel sound.

Notice the effect magic 'e' can also have on the letter 'g' in these word pairs:

> hug/ huge   rag/rage   stag/stage   wag/wage

It makes a long vowel sound but also makes the letter 'g' soft so that it sounds like 'j'.

Here are some other words where magic 'e' affects the vowel and the letter 'g':

> age   agent   courage   danger   digest   strange   stranger

Magic 'e' can have a similar effect on the letter 'c' too. When a 'c' is followed by an 'e', it changes to a soft, hissing 'ss' sound. Here are some words where magic 'e' affects the vowel and the letter 'c':

> ace   brace   disgrace   face   grace
> lace   pace   place   race   replace
> space   trace   dice   ice   lice
> mice   nice   price   rice   slice
> spice   twice   vice   puce   truce

LEARN: When the letters 'c' or 'g' are followed by an 'i' or 'y', they can also make a soft sound.

Some words have both a hard and soft 'c' sound:

accident   *access*   *concert*   *success*

Singulars and plurals

You need to know how to make **nouns** plural. Many spelling errors at 11+ English are made by forming incorrect **plurals**. There are some simple rules you can learn.

REMEMBER:
Singular means *one*; plural means *more than one*. Never make a word plural by using apostrophe *s*!

most plural nouns end in '–s':	*dog<u>s</u> chair<u>s</u> school<u>s</u> computer<u>s</u>*
nouns ending in a hissing sound like '–ch', '–sh', '–ss', '–s' or '–x', add '–es':	*church/church**es** wish/wish**es** glass/glass**es** bus/bus**es** box/box**es***
nouns ending in a consonant + y, change the '–y' to 'i' and add '–es':	*baby/bab**ies** berry/berr**ies** puppy/pupp**ies***
nouns ending in a vowel + y, add '–s':	*bay/bay**s** key/key**s** valley/valley**s***
nouns ending in –a or –o, add '–s' or '–es':	*camera/camera**s** piano/piano**s** echo/echo**es** tomato/tomato**es** potato/potato**es** hero/hero**es** solo/solo**s***
nouns ending in –f or –fe, change the –f or –fe to a 'v' and add '–es':	*shelf/shel**ves** scarf/scar**ves** life/li**ves***

LEARN: There are some exceptions to this last rule that just add '–s'. These need to be learned:

chef/chefs

belief/beliefs

chief/chiefs

handkerchief/handkerchiefs

LEARN: Look out for words that have irregular plurals, such as:

sheep/sheep	ox/oxen
salmon/salmon	child/children
woman/women	man/men
tooth/teeth	foot/feet
mouse/mice	deer/deer

LEARN: There are words that only have what looks like a plural form with 's' at the end. They are things which have two parts to them:

trousers, jeans, scissors, pliers, compasses, tweezers, pants, shears, and so on.

Common letter strings

Many words share the same common **letter strings** but some spelling patterns can be a little harder to learn. Learning and recognising these patterns can help you to say and spell unfamiliar words.

Some of the more challenging spelling patterns are shown in the tables that follow. Copy the 'torn off' lists into your own notebook to collect as many similar spellings as you can, and learn them. Especially learn the **exceptions** in the Learn boxes.

Sounds like 'er'

er	*ir*	*ur*	*ear*	*wor*
her	bird	purse	early	worth
certain	first	curl	learn	worm
term	girl	turn	earth	world

Sounds like 'or'

au	*augh*	*aw*	*oar*	*oor*	*or*	*our*
author	daughter	awful	soar	door	for	four
haul	taught	crawl	board	floor	story	court

LEARN: Watch out for these exceptions: *laugh, draught*.

LEARN: Here are some more letter strings that can make the same 'or' sound:

war: *warm* ('w' often changes the **vowel** sound in words)

ar: *quarter* (notice how when you say 'qu' it sounds like 'kw')

See also the table for letter string 'ough'.

This next letter string can be especially tricky, as it is pronounced very differently in different words.

ough							
Sounds like:	off	oh	oo	or	ow	uff	uh
	cough	dough	through	thought	bough	tough	borough

atch/etch/itch/otch/utch				
atch	**etch**	**itch**	**otch**	**utch**
batch	fetch	ditch	blotch	hutch
		kitchen		

LEARN: Look out for this set of words, which are spelled without a 't' but make the same sounds:

atta**ch**   ri**ch**   sandwi**ch**   whi**ch**   mu**ch**   su**ch**   tou**ch**

ack/eck/ick/ock/uck				
ack	**eck**	**ick**	**ock**	**uck**
lack	peck	pick	sock	luck
		sticker		

Spelling

adge/edge/idge/odge/udge				
adge	**edge**	**idge**	**odge**	**udge**
badge	hedge	fridge	dodge	fudge

cious/tious/xious		
cious	**tious**	**xious**
suspicious	cautious	anxious
vicious		

LEARN: Notice how words with the same sound can be spelled differently, such as brea*k*fast and te*ch*nique, and words borrowed from other languages such as tre*k* (Afrikaans) and wo*k* (Cantonese).

The letter strings in these words are especially difficult to learn. They all end in a 'shus' sound. As you come across other words like this, add them to the list.

Homonyms

These are words that are spelled exactly the same but have different meanings. Some are pronounced differently, depending on their meanings. These are called **homographs**.

Homonyms can cause confusion for readers. Sometimes you have to stress different syllables or change the vowel sounds to make the meanings clear. Look at these examples of homonyms:

Same pronunciation

bark/bark	block/block	club/club	fly/fly	form/form
jam/jam	leaves/leaves	train/train	watch/watch	waves/waves

Here are some sentences that show the different meanings of three of these homonym pairs:

Sam watched the *fly* *fly* past the window.

He was making a *bark* rubbing when his dog began to *bark*.

I ate a *jam* sandwich while sitting in the traffic *jam*.

REMEMBER: These same pronunciation homonyms are often different word classes. (See Section 19.)

HAVE A GO

3 In your notebook, write down similar sentences to the examples above for each of the other pairs of homonyms.

Different pronunciation (or homographs)

bow/bow   conduct/conduct   content/content   desert/desert
lead/lead   live/live   minute/minute   perfect/perfect
present/present read/read   row/row   sow/sow
tear/tear   wind/wind   wound/wound   Polish/polish
entrance/entrance invalid/invalid denier/denier

Do you know how each of these homonyms is pronounced?

Here are some sentences that show the different meanings of three of these homonym pairs:

The guide will **lead** you to the **lead** mine.

In a **minute** you will hear a **minute** splash as the stone hits the bottom of the well.

The nurse **wound** a bandage around the boy's **wound**.

HAVE A GO

4 Choose five other different homonym pairs from the list in the 'Different pronunciation (or homographs)' box and write similar sentences to show their different meanings.

Show them to an adult to discuss what you have written.

Silent letters and unstressed vowels

There are many words in English that have **silent letters** or **unstressed vowels** in them and you will need to pay particular attention to these, because simply sounding them out will not help you to spell them correctly.

On the next pages are some of the most common silent letters, with some handy hints that can help you think about where these letters can appear. Some useful silent letter words are given for each letter, but there are many more, so look out for them in your reading and writing. As you find them, add them to these lists.

Silent 'b' can come:
- before 't': debt, doubt, subtle
- after 'm': bomb, climb, comb, crumb, lamb, plumber, thumb, tomb, numb

Silent 'c' can come:
- after 's': descend, scene, scissors, science

Silent 'g' can come:
- before 'n': align, campaign, design, foreign, gnome, gnarled, gnat, gnaw, reign, sign
- before 'h': high, light, might, delight, weight, sigh, bright, height

Silent 'h' can come:
- after 'c': anchor, chaos, chemist, choir, psychology, school
- after 'g': ghastly, ghost, ghoul, spaghetti, dinghy
- after 'r': rhubarb, rhyme, rhythm, rhinoceros
- after 'w': whale, wheat, when, which, while, whistle
- before some vowels: vehicle, honest, hour, honour, heir

Silent 'k' can come:
- before 'n': knead, knee, knife, knight, knit, knob, knock, know, knowledge, knot

Spelling

Silent 'l' can come:
- before 'f': calf, half
- before 'k': chalk, talk, walk, yolk
- before 'm': balm, calm, palm, almond, salmon
- after 'ou': could, should, would

Silent 'n' can come:
- after 'm': autumn, hymn

Silent 'p' can come in: cupboard, raspberry, psychology, pneumonia

Silent 's' can come:
- between 'i' and 'l': island, aisle

Silent 't' can come:
- before '–le' ending: castle, rustle, thistle, wrestle
- before '–en' ending: christen, fasten, glisten, listen, moisten, soften
- at the end of foreign words: ballet, chalet

Silent 'w' can come:
- before 'r': wrap, wreath, wreck, wren, wriggle, wrinkle, wrist, write, wrong, wrote
- after 's': answer, sword

LEARN: Making up mnemonics (short sentences, rhymes or silly stories) can help you remember the silent and unstressed letters in words. For instance:

See **T**om at the back of the cas**t**le giving a whis**t**le.

The **w**rinkled **w**ren **w**riggled on the **w**recked **w**reath.

Autum**n**al describes the autum**n**.

A hym**n**al is a book of hym**n**s.

Try tracing over the silent letters with a silver pen to make them stick in your mind.

Being aware of the way some vowel sounds are almost silent in some words is also important for your spelling.

Unstressed vowels are not sounded clearly, as in the word 'benefit' (the second 'e' sounds like 'uh').

Often they are not pronounced at all, as in the word 'medicine' (the first 'i' is often 'swallowed').

Read these examples of the two types aloud. Listen to what happens to the unstressed vowels. (They are underlined.)

LEARN: Unstressed vowels often come in words that contain the letter patterns 'en' or 'er'.

'uh' vowels: astr*o*nomy   dand*e*lion   gramm*a*r   simi*l*ar   tel*e*phone

'swallowed' vowels: jewell*e*ry   fact*o*ry   short*e*ning   int*e*rest   mini*a*ture   fami*l*y

HAVE A GO

5 Read these words aloud to yourself. Find each unstressed vowel and highlight it.

boundary	business	conference	dangerous	definitely
dictionary	different	easily	extraordinary	eventually
favourite	generous	glamorous	heaven	history
humorous	interesting	occasionally		

Adding prefixes

You need to know the meanings of some of the most common prefixes as they may help you to understand the meanings of some unfamiliar words. Not all prefixes have particular meanings but you should know the most common ones:

> **LEARN:** A prefix is a group of letters added to the beginning of a word to change its meaning.

Prefix	Examples
auto– means self	automatic autograph autobiography
bi– or di– mean two or twice	bicycle dissect bilingual
circ–/circum– means about or round	circle circus circumstance
co–/con– means with or together	cooperate congregate conversion
pre– means before	predict prefix preface
re– means again	repeat rebuild replace
sub– means under	submarine submit submerge
tele– means far off or distant	telephone television telescope
trans– means across	transatlantic transform transport

These prefixes are all used to make antonyms (opposites). (See page 76.)

Prefix	Examples
anti– means against	anticlockwise antidote antiseptic
de– means making the opposite of	decode deform demist
dis– means not or making the opposite of	disappear dislike distrust
mis– means wrong or false	misbehave misplace mistake
non– means not or opposite of	non-fiction nonsense non-stick
un– means not	unable unfit unlikely

HAVE A GO

6 Collect as many words with these and other prefixes as you can in your notebook and make sure you know what they all mean. Notice that the same root word can have different prefixes and then mean quite different things.

Adding suffixes

You need to know the most common suffixes:

–able   –ed   –er   –est   –ful
–ing   –less   –ly   –ment   –tion

LEARN: A suffix is a group of letters added to the end of a word to change its meaning.

Some of these can be added without changing the spelling of the **root word** (for example, –ful, –less, –ment) but sometimes changes to the root word are needed. Here are some general rules that can help you to work out what these changes are and when they are needed. Remember: most rules have exceptions!

If the root word ends with a short vowel sound followed by a single consonant, double the consonant then add the suffix:

(See Doubling letters, page 90.)

For suffixes –er, –est, –ly or –ness:

If the root word ends with a 'y', change the 'y' to 'i' then add the suffix.

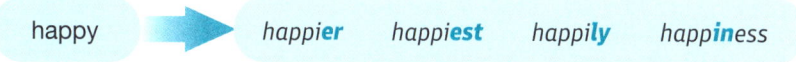

For the suffix –tion:

If the root word ends with an 'e', drop the 'e' then add the suffix:

If the root word ends with 't' or 'te', drop these letters then add the suffix:

Some root word endings will need to be changed further:

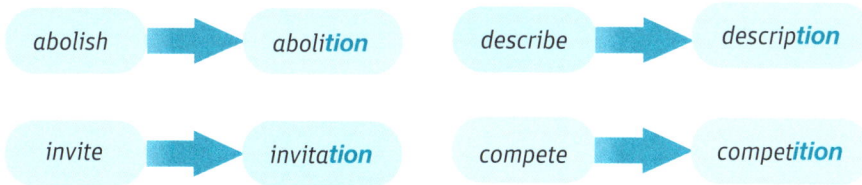

> **LEARN:** Here is the rule for adding suffixes to words that end in 'e': Ends in 'e', delete the 'e'!
>
> For suffixes beginning with an 'a', 'e' or 'i':
>
> If the root word ends with an 'e', drop the 'e' then add the suffix.

Some root words can take several different suffixes. Each suffix changes the meaning of the word.

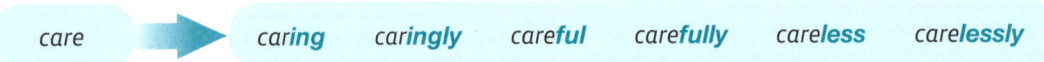

Sometimes the 'e' at the end of a root word needs to be kept before adding a suffix or else the meaning is changed. Notice what happens to these words if you drop the 'e':

'–shun' suffixes

Several different suffixes make the same 'shun' sound but they are all spelled differently.

Words ending in these letter strings can be rather tricky to spell:

–tion   –ssion   –cian   –sion (this last one often sounds a bit different from the others!)

Here are some rules to help you work out which is the right ending to use:

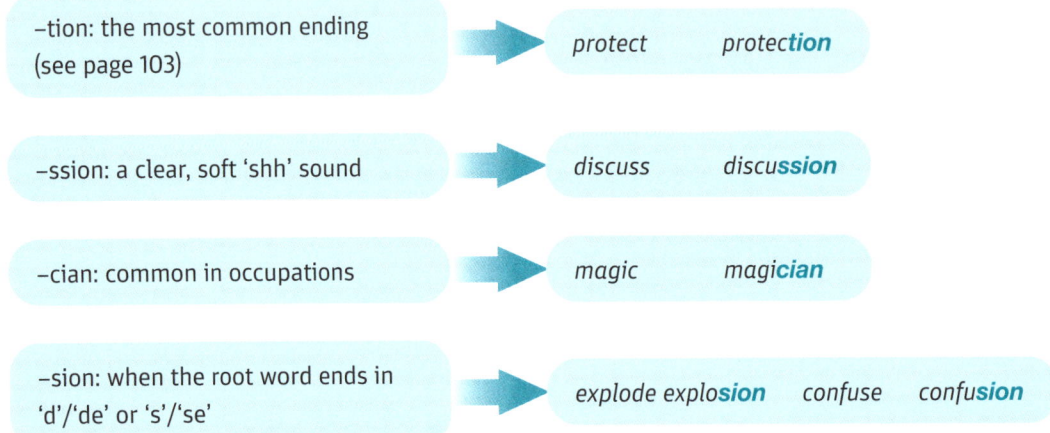

HAVE A GO

7 Sort these words into their suffix groups in your notebook.
Add more words to the groups as you come across them in your reading.
Split them into syllables to make learning their spellings easier.

competition	technician	devotion	translation	extension
possession	explanation	profession	direction	physician
fiction	collision	optician	musician	television
electrician	politician	commission	demonstration	

EXAM TIP

Don't worry too much about a word you know but are unsure of its spelling. It is better to write the word 'minicher' for *miniature* than to just write *tiny* as it shows you know the more interesting word and how to use it properly. Be brave and show what you know! Sound out the syllables and write these one by one for spelling multi-syllable words.

Skills builder

Try some of these activities to help improve your English 11+ skills, some at home, some out and about.

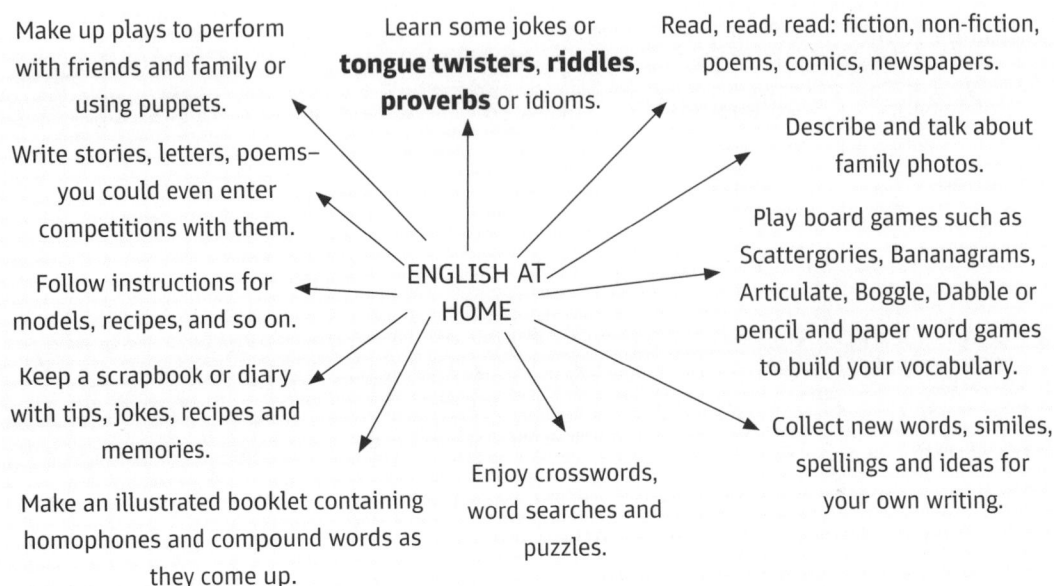

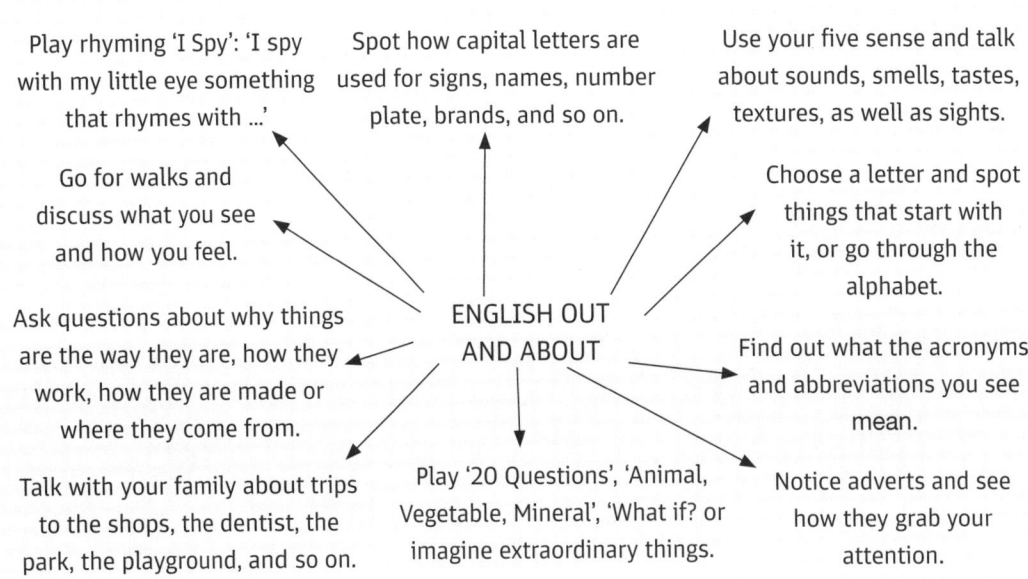

Skills builder

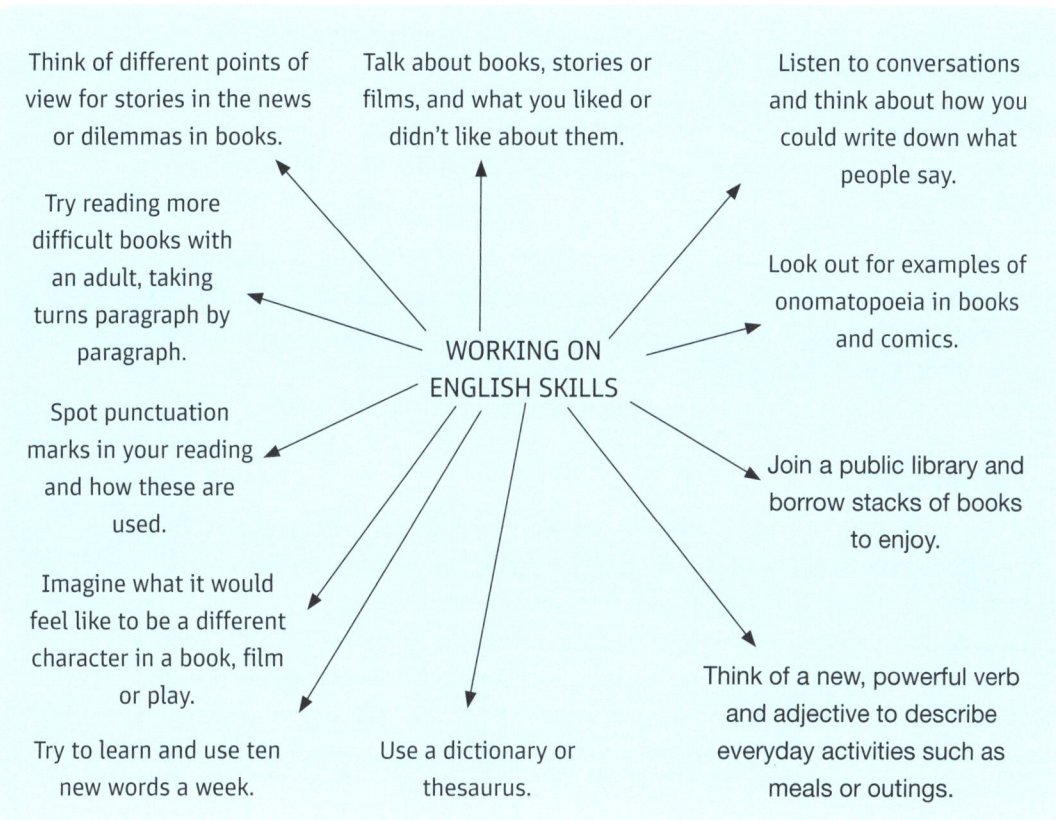

WORKING ON ENGLISH SKILLS

- Think of different points of view for stories in the news or dilemmas in books.
- Try reading more difficult books with an adult, taking turns paragraph by paragraph.
- Spot punctuation marks in your reading and how these are used.
- Imagine what it would feel like to be a different character in a book, film or play.
- Try to learn and use ten new words a week.
- Talk about books, stories or films, and what you liked or didn't like about them.
- Use a dictionary or thesaurus.
- Listen to conversations and think about how you could write down what people say.
- Look out for examples of onomatopoeia in books and comics.
- Join a public library and borrow stacks of books to enjoy.
- Think of a new, powerful verb and adjective to describe everyday activities such as meals or outings.

Study guide

You've worked through this book. Now test yourself!

1. Build confidence with practice

For more practice, and to put your skills to the test, work through the range of books and test papers in the Bond 11+ English range.

Mark your answers with an adult. Talk about the questions you got wrong or found hard to understand. Read the sections in this book again to help brush up on things you are still not sure about.

It is a good idea to go over examples of things that might come up in an 11+ English exam well before the date. A useful way to do this is to try some English tests that are similar to the exam you will be doing. The Bond Assessment Practice books and test papers, when used regularly, will provide useful, graded practice that will build your confidence and show you how well you cope with doing tests of this kind.

2. Time yourself

If you are just starting to prepare yourself, you may find it helpful to go through your first few Bond Assessment Papers in English untimed. This will help you to familiarise yourself with the types of questions and tasks you will face in the exam. Note down your scores (you could use the progress grids at the back of the Bond Assessment Practice books) and be sure to go over all the questions you found difficult until you understand them. After that, it is very important to give yourself a set time, just as you will have in the exam, so that you can practise pacing yourself and aiming to complete everything in the given time.

3. Revise strategies and techniques

It is also worth thinking about exam strategies and techniques. For many children, 11+ exams are the first exams they do in their lives, and they get very nervous at the thought of them. So do their parents! There are lots of hints on strategies and techniques in this book. Flick through them and talk about them to remind yourself. Highlight the ones that really work for you. It may be a good idea to make a reminder list of things to particularly look out for in the exam.

It is very important to remember that everyone is different. You will have your own way of coping and of doing things, which may be quite different from the way other people work. If you have worked through this book, you will have a good idea of your own strengths and weaknesses, the things you find easy or difficult. You will have developed your own strategies and techniques in tests and in your learning.

4. Prepare for the exam day

"I'm so nervous…"

Of course you may be nervous, but actually many people find they can enjoy their exams if they feel confident and well prepared. After all, you will have done the practice; now it's your chance to show what you can do!

Just before the exam

Here are some useful things to remember before the exam day arrives and on the day itself:

- ✔ Don't worry about feeling a bit nervous; that's natural. Most children will feel anxious. Talk about your feelings and try to relax.
- ✔ Plan something fun to do after the exam is over.
- ✔ Try to have a good night's sleep.
- ✔ Eat a healthy breakfast and have something to drink.
- ✔ Make sure you have what you need: pencil/eraser/ruler/sharpener/tissues/glasses/water bottle/inhaler, etc.
- ✔ Get to the place where the exam is happening in plenty of time.
- ✔ Find out where the toilets are and go if you can before the exam starts.

In the exam room

There should be no distractions during the exam because everyone is in the same boat as you and there will be at least one adult making sure that everything runs smoothly. The adult will tell you when to start the exam and when to stop. It is also their job to keep an eye on everyone and ensure there is no cheating.

However, there will be some distractions no one can do anything about. It could be a new, strange environment. It's your first real, public exam – and everyone else's too. People have distracting habits, like rocking their chairs, dropping things, muttering, fidgeting, sniffing… Some people may have a cough or a cold. Someone may need to go to the toilet. A child may not realise you can't ask for help and put up their hand to ask a question. Someone may have finished ages before you and is staring out of the window. It can all be very distracting! What can you do? The best thing is to ignore everything in the exam room apart from the adult in charge, the clock, the times written on the board and the exam paper in front of you.

Here are some useful strategies and techniques to remember once you are in the exam room:

- ✓ Keep calm. If you get butterflies or feel anxious, sit up straight, make sure your shoulders are not hunched and take some deep breaths. This allows plenty of oxygen to get to your brain, which needs it!
- ✓ Think positive. You've done all the hard work preparing. Now enjoy yourself!
- ✓ Find the clock. Make sure you know where it is before you start, so you can do a time check during the exam.
- ✓ Read the question. Not doing so is the most common mistake and easy to do something about.
- ✓ Write your answers carefully. Again, most mistakes are careless ones.
- ✓ Show what you know. This is your big moment and what you've practised for. Try to enjoy showing what you have learned.
- ✓ If you can't do a question, don't panic: have a go. Write something, and then put a mark in the margin, showing that you need to have another look if you have time at the end.
- ✓ Remember: a question left blank scores zero; a sensible guess may well be right.
- ✓ Leave time to check. Remember to leave a few minutes to check through your answers and make sure they make sense.
- ✓ Do your best: you can't do better than that!

GOOD LUCK!

Glossary

abbreviation – a shortened version of a word or **phrase**.
abstract noun – a feeling, concept or idea; something that cannot be seen, heard or touched.
acronym – the first letters of words put together as a short version and said as a single word.
active – where someone or something is actually doing something.
adjectival phrase – a group of words with the **adjective** as head of the **phrase**.
adjective – a word used to describe a **noun**.
adverb – a word usually used to describe a **verb**.
adverbial phrase – a group of words with the **adverb** as head of the **phrase**.
alliteration – the use of the same letter or sound at the beginning of words that are close together.
ambiguity – has more than one possible meaning; unclear.
antonym – a word with an opposite meaning to another word.
apostrophe – the punctuation mark (') used to show that letters have been missed out or to show that something belongs to someone.
auxiliary verbs – parts of the **verbs** 'to be' or 'to have' that go with other **verbs** to help make a **tense**.
character – a person in a story, play script or other kind of narrative text.
chronologically – in order of time passing.
clause – a simple **sentence** that has a **subject** and an active verb. It can stand alone or be part of a longer **sentence**.
cliffhanger – an ending to a story or piece of writing which leaves the reader guessing about what may happen next.
cloze test – an exercise in which you have to fill in gaps left in a piece of writing to test your understanding of it.
collective noun – a word that stands for a group or collection of things.
common noun – a word that is a general name for a person, place, animal, thing or event.
comparative adjective – the form of an **adjective** that expresses more in amount, degree or quality.
complex – a more complicated version of something.
compound word – two or more words put together to make a new idea.
conjunction – a word used to join together two or more **sentences**.
connective – a word or **phrase** used to join together two or more **sentences**.
consonant – a letter that is not a **vowel**.

context – the words that come before and after a particular word or phrase and help to fix its meaning.

contraction – when two or more words are joined together to make just one word, using an apostrophe to show any missing letters.

coordinating conjunction – a word to join two or more clauses or phrases of equal importance.

determiner – an article (*a*, *an*, *the*), a demonstrative (*this*, *those*, *that*), a number (*one*, *ten*, *thirty-six*), an ordinal (*first*, *next*, *last*), a possessive (*his*, *our*, *my*, *your*) and a quantifier (*all*, *none*, *some*, *every*) that is placed before a noun.

dialogue – a conversation between two or more characters in a story.

digraph – a group of two letters forming one sound, such as 'th' and 'ey'.

dilemma – a problem that needs to be solved.

diminutive – a small or young version of something or somebody.

direct speech – the actual words people say to each other.

double negative – saying 'no' twice, so that it means 'yes'.

ellipsis – omitting a word or words from a **sentence**, usually so that the sentence can still be understood.

exception – a word that does not follow common rules and needs to be learned separately.

feedback – advice and comments given by someone else in response to a piece of writing.

feminine – female, like a girl or a woman.

first person – using 'I' or 'we'.

formal – following rules; polite.

fronted adverbial – a word or short **phrase** that can be placed at the beginning of a **sentence** for effect and that contains an adverb.

gender – tells whether something is male or female.

grammar – the rules for putting words together to form **sentences**.

head word – a word forming a heading to an entry in a dictionary.

homograph – a word that is spelled exactly the same as another word but pronounced differently with a different meaning, for example *entrance* (the entry into a location) and *entrance* (to feel delight or wonder).

homonym – a word that sounds the same as another and is spelled the same but has a different meaning, for example *Park the car near the park*.

homophone – a word that sounds the same as another but has a different meaning and is spelled differently, for example *sale* and *sail*.

hyperbole – when people use using exaggeration to make a point.

idiom – a phrase that is often used to mean something which is not the same as the actual words.

imagery – words used to bring pictures into the reader's mind.

imperative – expressing a command or instruction.

indefinite pronoun – a word that stands for a **noun** but not a particular one.

indent – a way to show the beginning of a **paragraph** where the first line of writing begins a little further to the right of the **margin** than the other lines.

infer – work out meaning from the clues in a text, even though the exact meaning is not given.

infinitive – the name of a verb starting with *to*.

informal – being relaxed and chatty.

introduction – the beginning of a piece of writing, setting the scene or introducing characters or ideas.

inverted commas – the marks (" " or ' ') added before and after words spoken, also known as speech marks.

irregular – does not follow the usual rules.

Latin – an old language spoken by the Romans hundreds of years ago that forms the root of many English words.

layout – the way in which the parts of something are arranged on a page.

legibly – writing in a way that can be read easily.

letter string – letters that commonly go together to make certain sounds.

line space – leaving a line between paragraphs instead of using indents

main clause – part of a **sentence** that contains a verb.

margin – a blank border at the left-hand side of a page.

masculine – male, like a boy or a man.

metaphor – a word or **phrase** used to describe something as if it was something else.

mnemonic – a way of remembering things that are difficult to remember.

modal verbs – words such as *could, would, should, shall* and *might* that help modify other verbs.

moral – a lesson that stories like fables teach a reader.

narrator – the person telling the story.

negative – saying *no* or *not*.

noun – a naming word.

noun phrase – a group of words with a **noun** as head of the **phrase**.

object – who or what is being affected by the **subject** and the **verb** in a **sentence**.

onomatopoeia – forming or using words that sound like the thing they stand for, for example *cuckoo*, *plop*, *sizzle*.

onomatopoeic – sounding the same as its meaning. See **onomatopoeia**.

paragraph – a **sentence** or set of sentences describing one stage of a piece of writing, separated from the next paragraph either by a line space or an **indent**.

parenthesis – something extra that is put into a **sentence**, usually between brackets or dashes.

parts of speech – see **word class**.
passive – where someone or something is having something done to them.
personal pronoun – a word that stands for a **noun** and shows who or what.
personification – when non-human things are described or explained as if they were people.
persuasive writing – a piece of writing that tries to make the reader share a point of view.
phrase – a group of words that has a meaning but is not a complete **sentence**.
plot – the problem or dilemma developed in a story.
plural – more than one.
positive – saying *yes* or *definitely*.
possessive pronoun – a word that stands for a **noun** and shows to whom it belongs.
predict – decide what may happen next, using clues in the text to support what you say.
prefix – a group of letters added in front of a **root word** to change its meaning.
preposition – a word that shows the position, direction or timing of a **noun**.
pronoun – a word used instead of a **noun**: *he*, *it*, *they*, *we*, *you*, *she*, *I*, and so on.
pronunciation – how you say a word.
proper noun – a special name (or **title**) of a person, place or thing, that begins with a capital letter.
prose – a piece of continuous writing.
proverb – a wise saying, often from long ago.
recount – a retelling of a series of events.
relative clause – a clause that uses a **relative pronoun** such as *who*, *when*, *that*, *which* to join additional information to a **noun phrase**.
relative pronoun – a word that stands for a **noun** and tells more about it.
repetition – when words or phrases are repeated several times close together for effect and emphasis.
reported (indirect) speech – what people say to each other, but not in the actual words they use.
rhyme – a similar sound in the endings of words.
rhythm – a regular pattern of beats, sounds or movements.
riddle – a puzzling **sentence** or question that needs careful thought to work out.
root word – the main part of a word to which **prefixes** and/or **suffixes** can be added.
scan – to look quickly through a text.
sentence – a group of words that go together to make sense, usually starting with a capital letter and ending with a full stop.
silent letter – a letter that cannot be heard in a spoken word.

simile – a **phrase** used to compare one thing with another using *like* or *as … as*.
singular – only one.
Standard English – a form of English that is used as a guide for good English.
standard format – (of questions in a test, quiz, and so on) where the correct answer is written into the space provided.
stanza – a group of lines in a poem.
strategy – a way of working out a problem.
structure – the shape of a piece of writing and how it is organised.
subject – who or what is doing the action of the **verb** in a **sentence**.
subjunctive form – a **tense** that uses *were*, for instance, instead of *was* to express hopes, dreams or wishes.
subordinate clause – part of a **sentence** that adds meaning to the main clause but cannot be used as a sentence on its own.
subtitle – a heading for a shorter part of a longer section of text, often in newspapers.
suffix – a group of letters added after a **root word** to change its meaning.
superlative adjective – a word that is used to describe the most, the biggest, the best, the worst, and so on.
syllable – part of a word that contains at least one **vowel** and makes one sound.
synonym – a word with a similar meaning to another word.
technique – a way of doing things.
tense – used to show if a **verb** is in the past, present or future.
third person – using *he*, *she*, *they* or *it*.
time adverbials – adverbs such as *first*, *next*, *later*, *tomorrow* that help to structure time and order.
title – the name of a book, film, song, and so on; also a word used to show a person's rank or position.
tongue-twister – an amusing **phrase** or rhyme that is hard to say out loud.
topic – something to write, learn or talk about.
trigraph – where three letters are used together to make one sound, such as 'tch' or 'igh'.
unstressed vowel – a **vowel** that is not clear when a word is spoken.
verb – an action word that shows doing, having or being.
vocabulary – the range of words that a person knows and can use.
vowel – any of the letters *a*, *e*, *i*, *o*, *u* and sometimes *y*.
word class – any of the groups into which words are divided in **grammar** (**noun**, **pronoun**, **determiner**, **adjective**, **verb**, **adverb**, **preposition**, **conjunction**, exclamation).

Answers

3 Identifying different question requirements

a d or i
b f
c r
d f
e d or i
f r
g d or i
h d or i
i f

4 Defining words used in the text

1 D competing
2 D nauseated
3 machinery; fields; sow; harvest; farmers; animals

5 Cloze tests

1 boarded; dismay; squashed; corridor; between; still; reserved
2 a could have
  b seen anything
  c dripped off
3 farmer; children; sun; hours

7 Checking your answers

1 3
2 Time is passing too slowly.
3 clock striking; ticking clock; old beams creaking; stairs creaking; aunt's snoring
4 C recognisable
5 A small sounds made him think of ghosts
6 B he was afraid of waking Sid

11 Improving your writing

1–14 Answers will vary.

13 Other kinds of writing

Answers will vary.

15 Phrases and clauses

1 a s
  b p
  c s
  d mc
  e p
  f sc
  g sc
  h p
  i mc
  j mc
2 Answers will vary.

17 Commas

Arif, pleased with the progress they were making, decided to call for a break. "Let's grab a bite from the kitchen," he suggested, "and then, if you like, we can go out for some fresh air, exercise and a change of scene."

The others agreed and Aidan, suddenly remembering he had promised to phone his mother, made a quick phone call. "It's going really well, Mum," he said. "Tell Dad, Giles, Uncle Jamie and Ellie to be ready for six o'clock."

18 Other common punctuation marks

a–e Answers will vary.

19 Word classes or parts of speech

1 Common nouns: rattlesnake, football match, orchestra, soup, jelly, chimpanzee, pencils
Proper nouns: Sunday, Italy, Easter, Aunty Sue, Mr Jarvis
Abstract nouns: anger, sorrow, atmosphere
Collective nouns: a gaggle of geese; a pride of lions
2 Zak will enjoy his trip to the zoo because he loves animals.
3 A squirrel ate the bird food.
4 We had jumped on the trampoline.
5 Every day I try <u>to tidy</u> my room and <u>to prepare</u> my lunchbox for school
6 Sarah wasn't sure if she <u>should</u> go skating or not.

7 a <u>Yesterday evening</u>, I was (really) surprised to see a flock of <u>large</u>, <u>white</u> doves settle on the <u>next-door</u> roof.
  b (Each day) is <u>different</u> when we walk to school because they are building <u>new</u> houses along the <u>main</u> road.
  c Flip, Misha's <u>huge</u> <u>black</u> Labrador, was (frantically) chasing a <u>fluffy</u> <u>tabby</u> cat round the garden, barking (madly).
  d <u>After a lot of effort</u>, Kubi managed to complete his <u>enormous</u>, <u>complicated</u> jigsaw puzzle.
  e Bring along <u>warm</u> clothes, a <u>packed</u> lunch, a <u>small</u> notepad and two <u>sharp</u> pencils.
8 a They loved playing it.
  b It is mine.
  c She enjoyed it.
  d We visited them.
9 a–e Answers will vary.
10 <u>During</u> the Fun Run <u>in</u> the country park <u>at</u> the weekend, we had to go <u>through</u> mud, <u>over</u> fences, <u>under</u> hedges, <u>up</u> a hill, <u>down</u> a water slide and <u>across</u> a swampy field, getting <u>to</u> the end <u>before</u> lunch <u>at</u> 1 p.m.
11 Answers will vary.
12 a It was pouring with rain <u>after</u> the match was over.
  b <u>Although</u> she had forgotten her books, Eva didn't get told off.
  c Our cat was really ill last week <u>but</u> she has recovered now.
13 a After the match was over, it was pouring with rain.
  b Eva didn't get told off, although she had forgotten her books.
14 a every
  b friendship
  c into
  d while
  e luckily
  f larger
  g we
  h should
  i so
  j Manchester

20 Subjects and objects

1 a The bird (hopped) among the branches. It hopped among them.
  b Susie and I (collected) conkers. We collected them.
  c Our hockey team (won) the match. We won it.
2 a–c Answers will vary.
3 a–c Answers will vary.

21 Gender and diminutives

goose – gander – gosling
fox – vixen – cub
niece – nephew
waiter – waitress
cow – bull – calf
uncle – aunt
host – hostess
bride – groom
pig – sow – piglet

22 Synonyms and antonyms

Answers will vary but examples include:
1 a under
  b brave
  c smooth
  d early
  e end
2 a tired
  b simple
  c grinned
  d make
  e incorrect

23 Abbreviations and acronyms

Answers will vary.

24 Compound words

Answers will vary but some examples are: overcoat, football, waistline, snowball, underline.

25 Direct and reported speech

1.
   a. Dan said to his mum that he would like a party on his birthday.
   b. Mr Slater remarked that it felt like winter today.
   c. Charlie's grandad asked him to come inside and have a hot drink with them.
2.
   a. "Your behaviour is improving," the principal told the children.
   b. "I feel tired," complained my father.
   c. Rosie's mother asked her, "Did you remember the note from school?"

28 Learning awkward spellings

1. Making their way through the beech wood which led to the main sandy beach, Ahmed and Jake knew that they were only allowed to use the route that passed the golf course where their dads were having a practice game before the principal tournament of the season. The low beech branches caught at their hair so it took them a whole hour before at last they saw the coarse, waist-high grass of the dunes with the sea beyond.
"Nearly there!" shouted Jake. "Race you, Ahmed!"
"You're the winner," puffed Ahmed, as they reached the sand.
2. Answers will vary.
3. Answers will vary.
4. Answers will vary.
5. bound*a*ry; bus*i*ness; conf*e*rence; dang*e*rous; defi*n*itely; diction*a*ry; diff*e*rent; eas*i*ly; extra*o*rdinary; eventu*a*lly; fav*ou*rite; gen*e*rous; glam*o*rous; heav*e*n; hist*o*ry; hum*o*rous; int*e*resting; occasion*a*lly
6. Answers will vary.
7. –tion: competition, devotion, translation, explanation, direction, fiction, demonstration
–ssion: possession, profession, commission
–cian: technician, physician, optician, musician, electrician, politician
–sion: extension, collision, television, vision

Notes

OXFORD
UNIVERSITY PRESS

Great Clarendon Street, Oxford, OX2 6DP, United Kingdom

Oxford University Press is a department of the University of Oxford.
It furthers the University's objective of excellence in research, scholarship,
and education by publishing worldwide. Oxford is a registered trade mark
of Oxford University Press in the UK and in certain other countries

© Oxford University Press 2024
Written by Liz Heesom

The moral rights of the author have been asserted
Database right Oxford University Press (maker)

First published in 2024

All rights reserved. No part of this publication may be reproduced,
stored in a retrieval system, or transmitted, used for text and data mining,
or used for training artificial intelligence, in any form or by any means,
without the prior permission in writing of Oxford University Press,
or as expressly permitted by law, or under terms agreed with the appropriate
reprographics rights organization. Enquiries concerning reproduction
outside the scope of the above should be sent to the Rights Department,
Oxford University Press, at the address above

You must not circulate this book in any other binding or cover
and you must impose this same condition on any acquirer

British Library Cataloguing in Publication Data
Data available

ISBN: 9781382054157

10 9 8 7 6 5 4 3 2 1

Printed in the UK

The manufacturing process conforms to the environmental regulations
of the country of origin

Acknowledgements

Cover illustrations by Lo Cole
Typeset by Integra